STERLING BIOGRAPHIES

FREDERICK DOUGLASS

A Powerful Voice for Freedom

D0965093

Frances E. Ruffin

STERLING

New York / London
www.sterlingpublishing.com/kids

In loving memory of my parents, Frances and David C. Ruffin, Jr.

STERLING and the distinctive Sterling logo are registered trademarks of
Sterling Publishing Co., Inc.

Library of Congress Cataloging-in-Publication Data

Ruffin, Frances E.
  Frederick Douglass : rising up from slavery / Frances E. Ruffin.
     p. cm. -- (Sterling biographies)
  ISBN-13: 978-1-4027-4118-0
  ISBN-10: 1-4027-4118-9
  1. Douglass, Frederick, 1818-1895--Juvenile literature. 2. Abolitionists--United
States--Biography--Juvenile literature. 3. African American abolitionists--Biography--
Juvenile literature. 4. Antislavery movements--United States--History--19th century--
Juvenile literature. I. Title.

E449.D75R84 2007
973.8'092--dc22
  [B]
                                              2007019342

10 9 8 7 6 5 4 3 2 1

Published by Sterling Publishing Co., Inc.
387 Park Avenue South, New York, NY 10016
© 2008 by Frances E. Ruffin
Distributed in Canada by Sterling Publishing
c/o Canadian Manda Group, 165 Dufferin Street
Toronto, Ontario, Canada M6K 3H6

Distributed in the United Kingdom by GMC Distribution Services
Castle Place, 166 High Street, Lewes, East Sussex, England BN7 1XU
Distributed in Australia by Capricorn Link (Australia) Pty. Ltd.
P.O. Box 704, Windsor, NSW 2756, Australia

Sterling ISBN-13: 978-1-4027-4118-0 (paperback)
        ISBN-10: 1-4027-4118-9

Sterling ISBN-13: 978-1-4027-5799-0 (hardcover)
        ISBN-10: 1-4027-5799-9

Designed by Frieda Christofides for Simon Says Design!
Image research by Larry Schwartz

For information about custom editions, special sales, premium and
corporate purchases, please contact Sterling Special Sales
Department at 800-805-5489 or specialsalessterlingpub.com.

Contents

INTRODUCTION: From Slave to Freedom Fighter 1

CHAPTER 1: A Cabin in Tuckahoe 2

CHAPTER 2: A Child Slave at Wye House 7

CHAPTER 3: Growing Up in Baltimore 16

CHAPTER 4: A Slave's Life in St. Michaels 23

CHAPTER 5: Running North to Freedom 33

CHAPTER 6: A New Name in New Bedford 42

CHAPTER 7: Freedom Bought in Great Britain 56

CHAPTER 8: The *North Star* 62

CHAPTER 9: A Country in Turmoil 68

CHAPTER 10: War! War! 79

CHAPTER 11: Fighting for Military Equality 88

CHAPTER 12: Freedom Without Equality 97

CHAPTER 13: Fighting for Justice to the End 111

GLOSSARY 120

BIBLIOGRAPHY 121

IMAGE CREDITS 122

ABOUT THE AUTHOR 122

INDEX 123

Events in the Life of Frederick Douglass

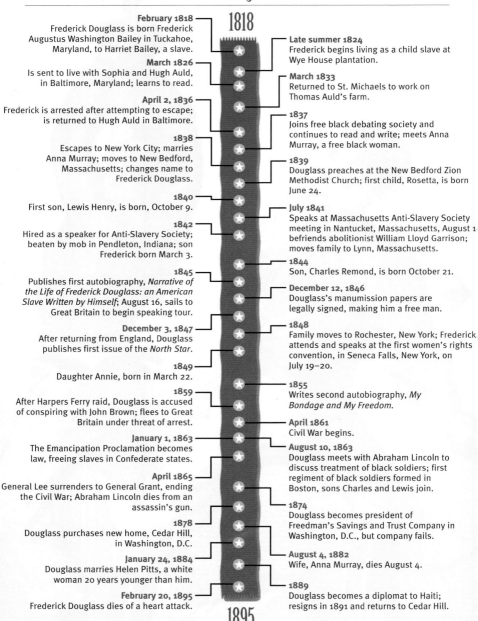

1818

February 1818
Frederick Douglass is born Frederick Augustus Washington Bailey in Tuckahoe, Maryland, to Harriet Bailey, a slave.

Late summer 1824
Frederick begins living as a child slave at Wye House plantation.

March 1826
Is sent to live with Sophia and Hugh Auld, in Baltimore, Maryland; learns to read.

March 1833
Returned to St. Michaels to work on Thomas Auld's farm.

April 2, 1836
Frederick is arrested after attempting to escape; is returned to Hugh Auld in Baltimore.

1837
Joins free black debating society and continues to read and write; meets Anna Murray, a free black woman.

1838
Escapes to New York City; marries Anna Murray; moves to New Bedford, Massachusetts; changes name to Frederick Douglass.

1839
Douglass preaches at the New Bedford Zion Methodist Church; first child, Rosetta, is born June 24.

1840
First son, Lewis Henry, is born, October 9.

July 1841
Speaks at Massachusetts Anti-Slavery Society meeting in Nantucket, Massachusetts, August 1 befriends abolitionist William Lloyd Garrison; moves family to Lynn, Massachusetts.

1842
Hired as a speaker for Anti-Slavery Society; beaten by mob in Pendleton, Indiana; son Frederick born March 3.

1844
Son, Charles Remond, is born October 21.

1845
Publishes first autobiography, *Narrative of the Life of Frederick Douglass: an American Slave Written by Himself*; August 16, sails to Great Britain to begin speaking tour.

December 12, 1846
Douglass's manumission papers are legally signed, making him a free man.

December 3, 1847
After returning from England, Douglass publishes first issue of the *North Star*.

1848
Family moves to Rochester, New York; Frederick attends and speaks at the first women's rights convention, in Seneca Falls, New York, on July 19–20.

1849
Daughter Annie, born in March 22.

1855
Writes second autobiography, *My Bondage and My Freedom*.

1859
After Harpers Ferry raid, Douglass is accused of conspiring with John Brown; flees to Great Britain under threat of arrest.

April 1861
Civil War begins.

January 1, 1863
The Emancipation Proclamation becomes law, freeing slaves in Confederate states.

August 10, 1863
Douglass meets with Abraham Lincoln to discuss treatment of black soldiers; first regiment of black soldiers formed in Boston, sons Charles and Lewis join.

April 1865
General Lee surrenders to General Grant, ending the Civil War; Abraham Lincoln dies from an assassin's gun.

1874
Douglass becomes president of Freedman's Savings and Trust Company in Washington, D.C., but company fails.

1878
Douglass purchases new home, Cedar Hill, in Washington, D.C.

August 4, 1882
Wife, Anna Murray, dies August 4.

January 24, 1884
Douglass marries Helen Pitts, a white woman 20 years younger than him.

1889
Douglass becomes a diplomat to Haiti; resigns in 1891 and returns to Cedar Hill.

February 20, 1895
Frederick Douglass dies of a heart attack.

1895

From Slave to Freedom Fighter

Slaves sing most when they are most unhappy. The songs of the slave represent the sorrows of the heart.

Imagine being born into a life in which neither you nor your family has the right to own a home or any other possessions. In fact, your parents would not even have the right to raise their own children. At any time, you or members of your family could be sold far away from what you knew as home. In this life, you would not be paid for the hard work you are forced to do, and if you refused to work, you could be severely punished by being beaten.

Born into slavery, this was Frederick Douglass's life until he ran away to freedom at the age of twenty. Despite a difficult early life, he became one of the most famous African Americans during the nineteenth century. He taught himself to read at a time when he and other black people could have been punished, even threatened with death for learning such a skill. He also became one of the most extraordinary public speakers of his time. Until the day he died, Douglass used his voice to fight for the rights of black people. He helped change the lives of those who had little or no hope for a life of freedom.

CHAPTER 1

A Cabin in Tuckahoe

I do not remember to have ever met a slave who could tell of his birthday. They seldom come nearer to it than planting time, harvest-time, cherry-picking time, spring-time, or fall-time.

In the 1500s, European slave traders brought captured African men, women, and children to the Americas to be auctioned, sold, and to work as slaves. By the 1700s, the southern colonies depended heavily on the agricultural labor of slaves, and by the end of that century, slave owners were among the wealthiest and most powerful people in the country. By the winter of 1818, there were more than one-and-a-half million black men, women, and children of

Before 1861, cotton was the most profitable crop grown on southern plantations. This 19th-century engraving shows slaves on a cotton plantation being watched by overseers.

African heritage in America. Most of these people in this still-new country were enslaved. They lived, worked, and struggled to survive on large farms, called plantations, in states of the American South.

In February of that year, Frederick Douglass was born a slave at Holmes Hill, a farm in Tuckahoe, Maryland, near the Eastern Shore of the Chesapeake Bay. At birth, Frederick was given the name Frederick Augustus Washington Bailey. His mother, Harriet Bailey, was a slave. During his lifetime, Frederick never learned the exact date of his birth, and he never truly knew who his father was. As a young child, he had heard whispers about the man who may have fathered him. That man was believed to be his mother's owner, Captain Aaron Anthony, a white man.

In February of that year, Frederick Douglass was born a slave at Holmes Hill, a farm in Tuckahoe . . .

Aaron Anthony, a former sea captain, owned three farms and thirty slaves, including Frederick's mother, Harriet Bailey, and her six children. Because Harriet was a slave, her children were also slaves. Harriet and the men and other women who worked for him, often in fear, called Captain Anthony "the old master." During this time period, slave owners were often referred to as "master." Anthony was also the clerk and business manager of Wye House, a large plantation.

Raised by Slave Grandparents

As a very young child, Frederick had no memories of his mother. Shortly after he was born, she was moved to work on a

Tobacco was the first crop grown on Caribbean island plantations but was replaced by a demand for sugar. This 1596 engraving shows slaves processing sugar cane.

nearby farm owned by Captain Anthony. It was the custom in some slave communities that mothers who were exhausted from working in their owner's fields or kitchens gave their babies and very young children to an elderly grandmother or aunt for raising. When elderly females were considered too old to work, they could still prove their value by bringing up the next generation of slaves.

Frederick was raised by his grandparents, Betsey Bailey, a slave, and Isaac Bailey, a free black man. Isaac was a sawyer who cut and sold trees for lumber. Betsy Bailey was born in Maryland. It is believed that Betsey's grandparents were Africans who were taken to work as slaves on British plantations in the Caribbean islands. Many of these slaves were brought to Maryland and sold there at auctions to tobacco farmers.

Slave Auctions

A great fear of every black person held in slavery was to be auctioned, or sold off, at a slave market. Slaves were considered to be property like livestock or pieces of furniture. A slave auction created a lot of attention. White buyers and curious people crowded the marketplace as auctioneers described the health, physical strengths, and talents of each person brought forward to be sold. Auctioneers might call out: "What are your bids for this strong field hand?" "This twenty-four-year-old woman is an experienced cook."

A few individuals, or hundreds of people—including entire families—could be put up for sale at a time. The largest slave auction in the United States took place in March 1857 at a racetrack in Savannah, Georgia, where 429 men, women, and children were auctioned off in two days. One family, a mother and her five children, was sold for $6,180 (about $12,916 by today's standards).

Families were often separated in slave auctions. The buyers in this 19th-century engraving are bidding on mothers and their children.

Husbands and wives could be taken from their families, sold, and sent to the farm of another slave owner miles away or even in another state. Parents and children, sisters and brothers were pulled from one another's arms at auction time. People were separated from their loved ones forever. It is no wonder that slave auctions were called "the weeping time."

Grandmother Betsey Bailey had five daughters who worked on farms away from the cabin. She was a loving parent to the collection of infants and small children she brought up. She was also a vastly capable woman. Her small cabin, built of clay, wood, and straw, was in a wooded area. It was surrounded by sandy soil, almost too poor for growing crops needed to feed her family. However, Betsey managed to cultivate a few crops, including sweet potatoes. She also wove strong fishing nets that she sold to local fishermen. She was an expert fisherwoman and she caught nets full of shad and herring that swam in nearby waters. Frederick remembered his life with Betsey as a time that was "spirited, joyous, uproarious, and happy." Unaware that he was surrounded by a life of poverty, the young child played and ran free in the woods surrounding his grandparents' small cabin.

As a young boy, Frederick Douglass was familiar with the type of landscape shown in this photograph of Tuckahoe, Maryland.

CHAPTER 2

A Child Slave at Wye House

[Aunty Katy] meant to starve the life out of me.

One very warm morning in August 1824, Betsey Bailey left her cabin with six-year-old Frederick firmly in hand. The old woman and little boy walked a southwest route that took them past wild meadows and fields cultivated for crops. They walked through forests that cooled them on that hot day. At times, Frederick glanced into the dark woods and thought he saw the eyes and teeth and legs of large animals that would eat him, only to find that they were faded logs and broken tree limbs. Still, they made Frederick grab his grandmother's long skirt.

They had walked twelve miles when they came into view of Wye House, the largest home that Frederick had ever seen. The great, pale yellow house with many windows that seemed to peer down at the old woman and child was the home of Colonel Edward

They had walked twelve miles when they came into view of Wye House . . .

Lloyd, a wealthy man who belonged to one of the oldest white families in Maryland. Wye House plantation was named for the Wye River that flowed nearby.

Beyond Colonel Lloyd's great house was the cottage of Aaron Anthony and his family. Behind that house were

Wye House

Wye House plantation had thirteen farms that were spread out over ten thousand acres. Crops on the land were planted and harvested by more than a thousand slaves. The names of these slaves were listed in the records alongside the other farm properties, including the hogs, cattle, horses, plows, and other farm equipment. In addition to the outbuildings, such as kitchens, laundries, hen houses, and stables that were found on most farms, there were many slave-run craft shops.

The property resembled a small village. There were blacksmith shops to shoe horses and cobblers to make and repair shoes for humans. There were weavers who made cloth, a mill for grinding grain, and a cooper's shop for making barrels. There was also a greenhouse. Few Americans in the 1880s had ever tasted the exotic fruits grown in this greenhouse. Wye House plantation has remained within the same family for more than 340 years. Today, descendents of some of the slaves who worked there still live nearby.

This 2006 photograph of the Great House at Wye House plantation shows an imposing view as young Frederick might have been seen it.

many crudely built cabins where the plantation's slaves lived. The trees around these cabins had been cut down so that from his cottage, Captain Anthony and anyone in the great house could keep watch over the men, women, and children who lived in the cabins.

The long trip had been tiring for Frederick, but after a cool drink of water in a kitchen building, he noticed a yard full of children playing. His grandmother led him to a boy named Perry, who was his older brother, and two girls, Sarah and Eliza, who were his sisters. They had come to Wye House when Frederick was too young to remember them. Betsey encouraged Frederick to leave the kitchen and join the children. Too shy to join in play, he watched the active youngsters. A short time later, a little boy ran up to him laughing and said, "Fed, Fed! Grandmammy gone!"

While Frederick's back was turned, Betsey had taken a final look at Frederick and slipped away. She had begun a sad walk back to her cabin before Frederick scrambled out to look for her on the road they had traveled. He could find no sight of Betsey. Heartbroken, his sense of loss was such that he could only sit in the yard and cry. He cried himself to sleep on his first night as a slave at Wye House, but it was not the last time that he would cry himself to sleep.

Somebody's Child

Frederick could not remember seeing his mother before the age of six. The four or five visits that she made to spend time with him occurred after he had begun living at the Wye plantation. In order to be with her child, Harriet Bailey completed her chores for the day. Then, just before dark, she began her walk of twelve miles to Wye House. She was not allowed to use a horse or mule from her master's farm to make that journey, and she had to make the twelve-mile return journey in time to begin another long day of work in the fields. Harriet's visits with Frederick always took place late in the evening in the Wye House kitchen building. She spent her time with her son, hugging and holding him on her lap. He was no longer the baby she had left in her mother's care six years before, but a long-legged young boy.

Frederick could not remember seeing his mother before the age of six.

Frederick was grateful for the attention that she gave him. He had missed his grandmother's warm, nurturing arms. Living at Wye House, he was often the object of strict discipline from the woman everyone called "Aunt Katy." She was a slave who ran the kitchen. Aunt Katy was a mean, short-tempered woman who took every chance she could to punish the lively young boy and other children as well. Her cruelty toward other slaves made her a favorite of their equally cruel owner, Captain Anthony.

One day, for reasons that are unknown, Aunt Katy punished Frederick by refusing to let him have any food. By dinnertime, he was so hungry that he picked out several hard kernels from an ear of Indian corn and placed them on hot ashes in the fireplace. As he was pulling out his kernels of corn to cool, his mother appeared on one of her rare visits.

Clothing Allowances

Once a year, adult slaves and older children were given two shirts made out of a rough linen fabric, a pair of linen trousers, and a linen jacket for summer, and a pair of woolen pants and a woolen jacket for winter. Each year they were supplied with one pair of stockings made of yarn and a pair of shoes. Once a year, children who were too young to work were given two long, coarse linen shirts that came to their knees. There were no shoes or stockings for them. When they wore out their shirts, some children went naked until the next clothing allowance. Slaves had no beds at Wye House plantation, but they were each given a coarse blanket in which to wrap themselves as they slept on the hard floor of their cabin. Some children slept near a cabin's chimney. Once the fires were put out for the day, they slept with their feet tucked into the ashes to keep warm.

This c. 1861 photograph captures three generations of a slave family wearing typical clothing of slaves and sitting in front of their cabin in Beaufort, South Carolina.

Harriet Bailey defends Frederick against the cruelty of Aunt Katy, as illustrated in this wood engraving from *The Life and Times of Frederick Douglass.*

Asked why he had no food, Frederick told her that Aunt Katy "meant to starve the life out of me." Harriet turned on Aunt Katy, threatening to tell their owner about the mistreatment of her son. Then, using Katy's kitchen, she made her son a ginger cake shaped like a heart. That evening, Frederick felt that he was "not only a child, but 'somebody's child.'" Wrapped in his mother's arms, he fell asleep. When he woke the next morning, she was gone.

That was the last time he saw his mother. Harriet Bailey died a year later, but it was a long time before he learned of her death. He knew little about his mother or her life. However, years later he was proud to discover that during her lifetime, she was the only black person in Talbot County who had learned to read. It is not clear how she had managed this feat.

Hungry and Cold

Not long after his arrival at Wye House, Frederick experienced other hardships of being a slave. He was always hungry. Once a month, adult slaves received eight pounds of salted pork or pickled herring and a large basket of cornmeal. Meals for Frederick and other children were mostly cornmeal that was boiled in hot water and stirred into a mush. The mush was poured on a long platter placed on the ground where the children knelt down and used oyster shells or other flat objects to scoop up the food as fast as they could to get their share.

Frederick was always cold during the winter months. He was given clothing that never kept him warm, and he slept on the dirt floor of a closet in Aunt Katy's kitchen to avoid the drafts that entered the cabin at night.

It was common for the slaves at Wye House—and at nearly every other place where people were enslaved—to endure brutal beatings that were given for a variety of charges, large or small. Some were disciplined for stealing food to help them stay alive. Others were severely punished when they tried to run to freedom. These beatings scarred their bodies, crippled, and sometimes even killed them.

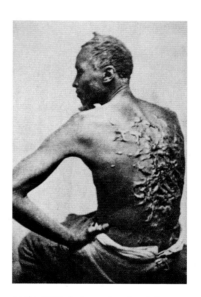

In this 1863 photograph, a freed slave shows the scars from many beatings.

Frederick witnessed how Captain Anthony brutally beat his slaves with a long piece of cowhide leather. One of Frederick's most heartbreaking memories was witnessing his aunt, Hester Bailey, hung by her hands with a rope, then beaten by Anthony. She was punished for slipping out one night to see the man she loved. Anthony also used whippings to keep other slaves in line if they appeared to disobey his orders. When that failed, "difficult" slaves were sold, sometimes to large cotton plantations farther south. On these large farms, slaves were worked harder and given harsher treatment. Being sold also meant leaving behind what family they might have had.

A Young Friend

In 1824, young Frederick was one of many children who could be seen playing in the yards near Wye House slave cabins. As they grew up in the slave system, some eventually learned a skill, such as carpentry or sewing, while others were sent to work in the fields. While six-year-old Frederick didn't have specific chores, he spent his time staying out of the way of Aunt Katy.

Frederick was a curious child, and he liked to wander the grounds of Wye House plantation. In time, he met and became the companion of Daniel Lloyd, a young boy who was five years older than Frederick and the youngest child of the plantation owner. It was not unusual to see the children of wealthy white families spend their days with a playmate-servant. Frederick and Daniel played, hunted, and fished together. For his part, "Master Daniel"—as Frederick called him— shared his cake and other treats with Frederick, and even stood up to older boys who might have tried to take advantage of his slave-companion. Frederick even sat nearby and listened when Daniel was given lessons from his tutor, a man who spoke in a cultured manner.

An 1863 wood engraving of domestic servants on a plantation. Young African American children often became playmate-servants of a plantation owner's children.

The Lloyds often had a house full of guests, and the comings and goings of Daniel and his young slave-friend in the grand house went unnoticed among them. Frederick was curious about the lives of the people who lived and visited Wye House. He wandered through rooms filled with beautiful furnishings and paintings and smelled the feasts being laid on the dinner table of the great house. He wanted to know who the guests were, what foods were being served, what kinds of serving dishes were used at the table, and what was said during meals. Unobserved, Frederick liked to listen to the Lloyds and their guests and often imitated the way they spoke.

In 1826, Captain Anthony, Frederick's owner, became ill and could no longer manage Wye plantation. He moved from Wye House and hired his slaves out to other farms. Most worked as field hands. Captain Anthony's daughter, Lucretia, who was married to Thomas Auld, had noticed Frederick and inexplicably felt protective about the boy who seemed special among the other slave children. He was bright and self-confident. She had some concern that the backbreaking work of planting and harvesting crops would be this eight-year-old boy's future.

Lucretia arranged for Frederick to be sent to live with her brother-in-law, Hugh Auld, and his wife, Sophia, in Baltimore, Maryland. Hugh was a shipbuilder in Baltimore. The couple had a two-year-old son, Tommy. Frederick could help Sophia Auld look after the child and run errands. Before Frederick left on his journey to Baltimore, Lucretia gave him his first pair of trousers and a tuck-in shirt.

CHAPTER 3

Growing Up in Baltimore

You will be free as soon as you are twenty-one, but I am a slave for life.

One morning in March 1826, Frederick settled into the *Sally Lloyd*, a sailboat that belonged to the Lloyds. In addition to the crew, his companions included a large flock of sheep. All were bound for Baltimore. A crewman named Tom, a cousin of Frederick's, looked out for the young boy as they sailed north on the Chesapeake Bay and stopped overnight at Annapolis, the state capital of Maryland. It was the first town that Frederick had ever seen. An even greater wonder greeted him when the boat sailed into the port at Baltimore.

A painted engraving, c. 1831, shows Baltimore Harbor as seen from the city's Federal Hill.

City Slaves

In his writings, Frederick Douglass noted that there was a marked difference in the treatment of slaves who lived and worked in the country from those who lived and worked in the city. "A city slave is almost a freeman, compared to a slave on a plantation," Douglass wrote. "He is much better fed and clothed, and enjoys privileges altogether unknown to the slave on the plantation."

Country slaves were housed in crude, often cold, slave cabins that had few pieces of furniture. Many city slaves lived in the homes of their owners, though most lived in basements or shared a stable with a master's horse and carriage. But unlike their country cousins, they had access to items of clothing and furniture that provided comfort. Many city slaves were able to acquire and use skills in a trade that enabled them to earn money on the side. For example, women learned to sew and became dressmakers while men learned shipbuilding trades. City slaves often went to the church attended by their owners, though some were permitted to attend black churches, which offered them the opportunity to meet and to develop relationships with free black people.

African American slaves in cities often lived more comfortable lives than those who toiled on farms. This 1861 wood engraving shows a Baltimore house slave and his mistress.

The sight of the large city overwhelmed Frederick. As he was being taken to the Aulds' house in the Fells Point area of the city, Frederick glanced around in awe at the large buildings, bustling crowds, and horse-drawn wagons. The city was noisy. The brick walkways raised blisters on his bare feet, but Frederick seemed not to notice. Sophia Auld, the lady of the house, greeted the young boy with a smile. That night he slept in his first real bed that had covers to keep him warm. At meals he was fed large helpings of bread and whatever foods the rest of the family ate. Sophia and Hugh Auld treated Frederick as another child in their household. Frederick earned his keep by taking young Tommy for walks, making sure to keep the child out of the way of bustling crowds and carriages. Frederick also ran errands for Mrs. Auld.

Sophia had come from a poor family and, before she married Hugh, she had never been around slaves. She treated Frederick as though he were an older brother to her son, Tommy.

A 19th-century wood engraving shows young Frederick Douglass being taught the alphabet by his mistress, Sophia Auld.

She took every opportunity to include him in family activities, including reading her Bible to the boys every day. Tommy sat on her lap while Frederick sat by her side.

As he listened to Sophia read, Frederick tried to make out what he later called "this mystery of reading." He memorized entire passages of the Bible, which made Sophia proud that he wanted to learn. With her assistance, he soon mastered the alphabet and three- and four-letter words.

An Angry Warning

Sophia, proud of Fredrick's progress, showed his accomplishments to Hugh. Auld immediately scolded her, saying that once a black man learned to read the Bible, "It would forever [make him unfit] for the duties of a slave." Auld raged on: "He should know nothing but the will of his master, and learn to obey it."

Eager to obey her husband's warning, Sophia suddenly changed from being the warm and tenderhearted woman who had enjoyed seeing Frederick as a young student, to becoming a short-tempered person, watchful that he not read any of her books. Whenever she caught Frederick with a book or a newspaper, she angrily snatched it from him. However, Frederick was determined to learn to read, and he used several clever ways to achieve this goal.

One way was to befriend a group of white neighborhood boys who were his age. Although many of them were poor, they still attended school. They knew Frederick's position in the Auld household, and they were curious about what it meant to be a slave. So Frederick would describe how the slaves at Wye House lived. His comment that "You will be free as soon as you are twenty-one, but I am a slave for life" troubled the boys.

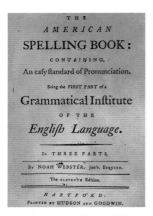

THE
AMERICAN
SPELLING BOOK:
CONTAINING,
An eafy ftandard of Pronunciation,

Being the FIRST PART of a

Grammatical Inftitute
OF THE
Englifh Language.

In THREE PARTS.

By NOAH WEBSTER, Jun'r, Esquire.

The ELEVENTH Edition.

HARTFORD:
PRINTED BY HUDSON AND GOODWIN.

Early American school children learned new words from a Webster's spelling book. Frederick Douglass always kept his copy of the book in his pocket.

Whenever Frederick was sent out on an errand or when the Aulds allowed him some playtime, he would tuck a small Webster's spelling book that he had found into one pocket and a biscuit into the other. After quickly completing his task, he would spend the rest of the time asking one of his young friends for a reading lesson. He paid for the lessons in biscuits, which were hungrily devoured by his young teachers.

By the age of twelve, Frederick was able to read most of the books that he picked up. From time to time, he also earned small tips for running errands or by shining the shoes of gentlemen on the busy streets of Baltimore. When he had fifty cents, he went to a bookstore and bought a book titled *The Columbian Orator*. His schoolboy friends read the same book for their class in school. It contained orations, or great speeches, made by famous people all the way from ancient times up to George Washington. Fredrick was delighted with this special prize that he had earned.

Whenever he had a free moment, he took the book to a deserted shipyard in Fells Point and read aloud speeches from its pages. Reading aloud helped Frederick understand the wisdom of the great men who had originally made the speeches. These men had dealt with such topics as freedom, the rights of man, American liberty, and even the institution of slavery. The ideas in the book later served as the basis for lectures that Frederick gave when he became one of America's greatest **orators.**

Free and Educated

In 1833, fifteen-year-old Frederick had become a tall and a powerfully built young man. He began to work for Hugh Auld in his shipyard. His duties included keeping watch over the shipyard while the carpenters went to dinner. The job also gave Frederick an opportunity to learn to write. He observed the carpenters marking pieces of timber with chalk. When the workmen went to dinner, Frederick used the chalk to write words on a fence and a brick wall. He also used to copy words from his Webster's spelling book. He developed his handwriting from **copybooks** that young Tommy Auld, now a schoolboy, had carelessly laid aside.

The job also gave Frederick an opportunity to learn to write.

Having heard the Bible read by Sophia Auld during his earlier years, Frederick was strongly influenced by religion as a young man, and he had begun to attend services at the Dallas Street Methodist Church. This was one of Baltimore's many Methodist and Baptist churches that drew the city's free people of color. He was attracted to the church because a frequent speaker was Dr. Lewis G. Wells, a physician. Wells was the first educated black man whom Frederick had ever met. Douglass also became acquainted with several of the young free men who attended the church and with Charles Lawson, a minister he called "good Father Lawson." When he heard his new friends speak of the evil of slavery, Frederick thought of the possibility of a life beyond slavery.

Frederick had become more outspoken, and Hugh Auld noticed the change. He was concerned about his young slave's new, bold behavior. Hugh wrote to his brother Thomas Auld suggesting that it would be in Frederick's best interest to return to the Maryland countryside and live on Thomas's farm, which was close to the town of St. Michaels and near the Lloyd plantation. Frederick's first owner, Captain Aaron Anthony, had died several years before, and his property, including his slaves, was divided between his son Andrew and his daughter, Lucretia. Upon the division of property, Lucretia became Frederick's mistress, or owner. When she died in 1827, her husband, Thomas Auld, took ownership of Frederick and became his new master.

Frederick was saddened and angry at being forced to leave Baltimore. He had matured during his seven years there. He had made friends, independent of the Aulds, and he had sniffed the promise of freedom in the air of that city. In the spring of 1833, Frederick sailed southward on the *Amanda* to the village of St. Michaels and watched steamboats sail north, a journey that he yearned to make one day.

A landmark sign in St. Michaels, Maryland, describes Frederick Douglass's life and where he lived.

CHAPTER 4

A Slave's Life in St. Michaels

*Having fought back, I gained the self-confidence
and determination to be a free man.*

At Thomas Auld's farm, Frederick once again came to live
the life of a slave in the country. He was one of four
slaves who worked in the kitchen of Auld's house. The
others included his aunt Priscilla, his cousin Henny, and
his sister Eliza. His sister Sarah had been sold to a cotton

A c. 1860 photograph of a cotton field in Savannah, Georgia, shows small
children working alongside adult slaves in the fields.

farmer in Mississippi. He later learned that many of his relatives had been sold to cotton plantations in the **Deep South**.

His new owner, Thomas Auld, had remarried a woman named Rowena. Unlike Lucretia, who had been a kind woman, Auld's new wife was given to cruelty. She encouraged her husband to beat cousin Henny daily. Because Henny's hands had been seriously disfigured in an accident, Rowena Auld claimed that Henny was unhelpful around the house. Thomas himself was a mean and stingy man. The couple gave their slaves very little food to eat, but they expected a long day of hard work. Each week the slaves were dealt out a small portion of cornmeal and nothing else—no meat or fish or vegetables. While extra supplies of meat and other foods meant for the Auld family lay spoiling in a locked food pantry, Thomas and his wife refused to share any of it with their workers who were always pinched with hunger.

It was also at Auld's farm that Frederick became a victim of severe beatings from his owner. One of Auld's horses had the habit of wandering into the pasture of the neighboring Hamilton farm. When Frederick went to retrieve the horse, the kindly cook at the farm wouldn't let the starving young man leave without filling his pockets with bread.

Thomas Auld discovered that Frederick allowed the horse to get loose on purpose so that the cook would give him food. This enraged Auld, who brutally beat Frederick.

Under the Whip of a Slave Breaker

After giving the young man several of these beatings, Auld decided that Frederick needed to change his independent city ways. He hired out his young slave to a man named Edward Covey, who owned a small farm. Covey was known as a "slave breaker." He was a man who was thought to be able to break the will of any rebellious slave. Using harsh tactics, Covey thought any slave working in the fields of his farm would not dare rebel against him—unlike the famous slave Nat Turner, who had organized a slave revolt several years before in 1831.

Slaves who were thought to be sullen, angry, or in general who misbehaved, were sent to Edward Covey. This exceptionally cruel man beat the men and women who worked on his farm, often **humiliating** them in a manner that would force them to defend themselves and, in turn, provoke more whippings. Even illness was no excuse for not working in Covey's fields. They all worked from early morning, under the hot afternoon sun, until the chill of nightfall.

Frederick had been at Covey's farm only a short time when he was ordered to drive a cart and a team of untamed oxen to pick up a load of wood. Having no experience in driving a team of large animals, Frederick lost control of the oxen, which crashed into a thicket of trees. Frederick barely escaped injury. After righting the cart and oxen, he collected the wood. On his return, the ox team rushed through a gate, again nearly crushing him.

When he explained his near-death accident to Covey, the man ordered Frederick back to the woods. Shivering in the

Heavy loads on farms were hauled by teams of oxen, as shown in this 19th-century colored engraving.

Nat Turner's Revolt

Slave owners like Edward Covey were in constant fear of slave uprisings, and while numbers of such revolts by slaves were planned, few occurred. The Nat Turner rebellion in 1831 was one that actually happened. Turner was a self-taught slave from Southampton County, Virginia. On one occasion, he ran away from his master, but he decided to return and lead others to escape from bondage.

This 19th-century engraving shows Nat Turner and his men planning their rebellion against slave owners.

On August 21, 1831, Nat and a band of slaves killed sixty white slave owners and their families before being shot by state and federal troops. The lawmen killed more than a hundred slaves during the conflict. Later, thirteen slaves and three free black men were hanged. Nat Turner escaped during the struggle, but he was captured on October 30 and was executed. Thereafter, Nat Turner's revolt caused several communities in the South to secure their towns against another revolt. Many African American slaves who had heard of Turner believed that he and his men were great freedom fighters.

raw January wind, Frederick watched as Covey walked to a tree and with an axe cut three switches, which he neatly trimmed with a knife. Then he ordered Frederick to remove his clothing. Frederick refused to do so, and Covey, "with the fierceness of a tiger," tore the young slave's clothes off and started to beat him.

Fighting Back

During the first six months at Covey's farm, Frederick was rarely free of lashes from Covey's whip—until the day he fought back. Near the end of a long and very hot day, Frederick was suddenly seized with a violent headache and collapsed. Seeing him lying in the field, Covey ran up to Frederick and kicked him in the head and left him there, bleeding.

A 19th-century card titled "The Lash" shows a black man bound and being whipped by his overseer.

When Frederick could stand, he walked to his owner Thomas Auld's farm to ask for his protection against Covey. Auld refused, saying he could spend the night but that he must return to the Covey farm the next day. Frederick left the next day, without having been given dinner the night before, or breakfast that morning.

After returning to the Covey property, he was in a barn preparing for the day's work when Covey entered with a large rope. Seeing anger in Covey's eyes, Frederick knew that he had to protect himself.

Covey struck him twice across the chest with a knotted whip. Frederick grabbed Covey and the two men fell to the ground, wrestling in the dirt. The men fought, exchanging blows for two hours. Other slaves on their way to chores watched in disbelief at the scene of a black man fighting back against a white man. Covey asked for assistance to hold Frederick down from various slaves who came and went in the barnyard, but all pretended they didn't understand him and went about their business. Finally, exhausted from fighting, Covey stopped, realizing that Frederick would never give up.

From that time until Frederick left the farm six months later, Covey never laid a hand on Frederick again. "I was a changed being after that fight," Frederick later wrote. "I was nothing before; I was a man now. Having fought back, I gained the self-confidence and determination to be a free man."

Freeland's Farm

In January 1835, Thomas Auld hired Frederick out to another farmer, William Freeland, who purchased Frederick from Auld to work for him for a year. Frederick's life improved greatly there. He was given enough food to eat and enough time to eat it before setting out to work. Mr. Freeland gave his workers reasonable work hours. During the year spent at Freeland's, Frederick was never whipped. Frederick claimed that William Freeland "was the best master I ever had, until I became my own master."

Frederick developed a close friendship with several men who worked on Freeland's farm. They included two brothers, Henry and John Harris, who were slaves owned by Freeland, a man named Handy Caldwell, a slave who was hired from another slave owner, and Sandy Jenkins, a free black man. Frederick organized a Sabbath school in the woods on Sundays at which he also taught the men to read. At first, only his friends attended, but when word spread, as many as thirty men showed up. Meetings were held secretly. During cold weather, they met in the home of a man whose name Frederick never revealed for that man's safety. Some of the men showed up with spelling books that their owners' children had thrown away. So popular was the class on Sundays that Frederick also held classes three evenings a week.

Despite his friendships and improved work conditions, Frederick began to suffer from a personal struggle. He was not content to live out his life as a slave. He would soon be an adult, and he was aware that he would do almost anything to

Most African American slaves held prayer meetings in secret. Slave owners feared that their slaves would learn to read from Bible studies.

gain his freedom. He was also determined to help the men who were his friends to find new lives as well.

As months passed, Frederick shared his thoughts of leaving Freeland's with John and Henry Harris. During their discussions, the word "escape" was whispered as a wishful idea, but in time, *escape* was no longer a word but a real plan. He described his plan with the Harris brothers, Sandy Jenkins, and two other slaves, Charles Roberts and Frederick's uncle, Henry Bailey.

The Betrayal

The six men planned to steal a large canoe owned by William Hamilton, a nearby farmer who used the boat for oyster fishing, and paddle north on the Chesapeake Bay. Having talked with boat workers on the docks of Baltimore, Frederick knew that by paddling north they would pass through a canal that crossed into the Delaware River. From there they would reach Pennsylvania, then New Jersey and New York—all states where owning slaves was illegal.

Frederick also knew along the way that he and his fellow escapees would be questioned about the purpose of their trip. Where were they going? Were they slaves or free men? And what was the purpose of their trip? To avoid trouble, he wrote passes for each man to hide and carry on his person, and he signed it in the name of William Hamilton:

> *This is to certify that I, the undersigned, have given the bearer, my servant, full liberty to go to Baltimore and spend the Easter holidays. Written with mine own hand, &c., 1835*
> *William Hamilton*
> *Near St. Michael's in Talbot County, Maryland*

On the evening of April 1, 1836, Frederick and the other men prepared for their journey by each setting aside a bundle of food and extra clothing. The next morning Frederick performed his early morning chores, but he had an uncomfortable feeling that something was wrong. Did William Freeland know what he planned to do? Had he and his friends been betrayed?

His fears were confirmed when he saw a posse, a gathering of armed white men riding on horseback. The group included Freeland and his neighbor William Hamilton. Frederick's

Slaves traveling without their owners were required to carry a pass, such as the one shown here, to explain the purpose of their journey.

uncle, Henry Bailey, and Charles Roberts were tied behind the posse's horses with heavy ropes. Frederick and the Harris brothers were rounded up and tied, as well. Missing from the group was Sandy Jenkins. The five men were tied and pulled along for fifteen miles behind the horses of their captors. When they reached the town of Easton, they were thrown into jail. During their long march. Frederick had whispered that the men should eat the passes that he had written. He hoped to destroy any evidence that would reveal their plans.

Once the men were jailed, Frederick and his fellow prisoners discussed who might have revealed the plot. Everything pointed to Sandy Jenkins. Frederick and the other men had a great respect for Jenkins, so they decided to "roll the guilt on other

This 1882 wood engraving from *The Life and Times of Frederick Douglass* illustrates his friend Sandy Jenkins, who might have been the one to betray Douglass.

shoulders," and preferred to think that the betrayer was someone other than Jenkins. All of the men, except for Frederick, were returned to the farmers who owned or hired them. However, Frederick was kept in jail for a week. He was thought to be a dangerous slave. Indeed, groups of slave traders had gathered around the jail in the hopes that they could buy the attempted escapees from their owners.

Frederick was terrified that he would be sold to work on one of the cotton plantations in Georgia, Alabama, or Louisiana. What was worse, several slave owners in the community wanted to have this rebellious bunch killed. At first, Frederick's owner, Thomas Auld, planned to sell him to a friend in Alabama but changed his mind. Instead, Auld decided to save Frederick's life by sending him to live, once again, with his brother Hugh Auld in Baltimore, where he could learn a trade to become a skilled laborer. Frederick would turn his earnings over to Hugh. What's more, Thomas Auld told Frederick that, if he stayed out of trouble, he would free Frederick when he reached the age of twenty-five years. It is not clear what motivated Auld to this act of kindness.

CHAPTER 5

Running North to Freedom

A free state around me, and a free earth under my feet! What a moment was this to me!

Frederick was grateful to return to Baltimore. Hugh Auld had made an arrangement with William Gardiner, a Baltimore shipbuilder, to hire Frederick as an **apprentice** to work in Gardiner's shipyard. Almost all of Frederick's wages, $6–$9 a week, were turned over to Hugh Auld.

At the shipyard, Frederick was to be ready to assist more than one hundred skilled carpenters and other laborers. He felt that he needed a dozen hands to do his job as the men called out all at once: "Fred, come carry this timber yonder." "Fred, go get a fresh can of water."

This 1840 wood engraving of a shipyard resembles the Gardiner shipyard where Frederick Douglass worked.

Frederick was a hard worker, but many of the white workers resented him. They feared that shipbuilders would begin to use slave labor that was free or was paid low wages, and the white workers would lose their jobs. Sometime before Frederick started on the job, white carpenters had held a strike forcing the shipbuilder to fire the free black men who were skilled carpenters. Because of this issue, Frederick endured angry racial comments until one day four men beat him badly.

Hugh Auld found another builder to hire Frederick as an apprentice caulker. He would learn an important skill in those seagoing days. Caulkers filled in the seams of boats to make them watertight. This was done by soaking rope in a tar mixture, then pounding the wet rope into the cracks between wood planks in the hull or body of the ship.

Frederick was a hard worker, but many of the white workers resented him.

His new job also gave him a new confidence and a desire to be his own man—at least economically. By the spring of 1838, Frederick made a deal with Hugh Auld that, in addition to his work as a caulker, he be permitted to find his own part-time employment. In return for this privilege, he would pay Hugh three dollars a week from this extra work, though Frederick would have to pay the three dollars whether or not he found work that week. He would also find his own place to stay and pay for his own food and shelter, clothe himself, and buy his caulking tools. His goal was to save enough money to buy his freedom. With freedom came **manumission** papers, which every free black person carried. Without this proof of freedom, they risked being enslaved again.

The Friendship of Free Men

Baltimore was becoming a beacon city for free people of color. When plantation owners freed their slaves, the ex-slaves headed for Baltimore as free blacks and the opportunity of finding paying jobs. Frederick befriended several caulkers who were free black men and belonged to a group called the East Baltimore Mental Improvement Society.

Although only free men were allowed to belong to the society, they permitted Frederick to join because he could read and write, and he was greatly admired by the society's members. The men read and wrote and calculated math with ease. For the first time, he was no longer the only black man in a group who was able to read a book. The group held debates on a variety of subjects, although the topics of these debates usually dealt with slavery. Frederick later gave credit to the society for helping to develop his skills as a commanding speaker and debater. The group also had musicals, where Frederick played the violin. Though he was untrained, it is believed that he had had a few lessons, and he continued to improve on his own. He enjoyed playing music for the rest of his life.

Shown is the violin owned by Frederick Douglass, who learned to play the violin as a young man. Many years later he was delighted when his grandson, Joseph Douglass, became a concert violinist.

Free Blacks in Maryland

Free black people had lived in Maryland as early as the 1600s. African American slaves were given their freedom for a variety of reasons. Some owners stated in their wills that upon their deaths their slaves would be emancipated, or granted freedom. Others rewarded their slaves' freedom after many years of hard work and loyalty. A slave could also buy his freedom for as much as $1,000 or more. Few slaves could afford the price. One of the most famous free black men in Maryland was Benjamin Banneker, who was born in 1731 and was a scientist, an inventor, and a writer. George Washington hired Banneker to help lay out the plans for the nation's capital city, Washington, D.C.

Maryland law declared that children born to a free mother were also free. By 1830, about 53,000 black people in the state were free, though life was not easy for these former slaves. They did not have the same rights as white citizens. They were not permitted to vote, and they were limited to jobs that white workers would not do. More troubling, freed blacks were often in danger of losing their freedom from slave catchers who would capture them and sell them back into slavery. To protect themselves, the free black people in Baltimore formed the Maryland **Abolition** Society.

Benjamin Banneker, a free black born in 1731 in Maryland, was a scientist, a mathematician, and an astronomer.

In 1837, Frederick met Anna Murray at one of the society's meetings. She was a free woman whose family had come from eastern Maryland, and she worked as a servant in the household of a wealthy family. Anna was a plain-looking woman who was about five years older than Frederick. Although they had met at a society meeting, Anna was uneducated and could neither read nor write. However, she admired Frederick and supported his interests. She was also a hardworking, religious,

This is a portrait of Anna Murray Douglass, who married Frederick Douglass in 1838 and became the mother of their five children.

and thrifty woman. These were values that Frederick admired. During the summer of 1838, twenty-year-old Frederick yearned to be part of a family again. He thought about marriage to Anna and of starting his own family.

A New Plan

Frederick's new achievements made him even more dissatisfied that he was a slave. Although his owner, Thomas Auld, had promised Frederick that he would free him when he reached his twenty-fifth birthday, Frederick didn't believe that Auld would live up to that agreement. Hugh Auld had also insisted on Fredrick moving back into his Baltimore household, which made Fredrick worry that he might be sold. Once again, the thought of running away, and leaving Maryland—and soon— was on Frederick's mind. It would be difficult to leave behind his new friends and Anna. He was also concerned that as a fugitive, or runaway slave, he could be killed or sold to slave traders. Yet, none of these thoughts discouraged him.

On September 3, 1838, Frederick tucked away money that he had borrowed from Anna to buy a train ticket to Delaware. It was said that she had sold her featherbed to give Frederick the money for his escape. Dressed as a seaman, in a red shirt, black kerchief, and a sailor's hat, Frederick jumped on a northbound train. He walked toward the "Negro car" and sat down holding his breath as the conductor collected tickets and looked at the papers of each black passenger. Frederick had borrowed a set of seaman's protection papers from a free black sailor who was retired. Seamen carried these papers when they landed in foreign ports. The papers did not match Frederick's description, but the conductor did not give him a second glance.

Continuing his northbound journey, Frederick took a steamboat from Wilmington, Delaware, to Philadelphia, Pennsylvania, then a train to New York City. He was thrilled when he arrived in New York. "A free state around me, and a free earth under my feet! What a moment was this to me!" he thought. But this carefree feeling was short-lived.

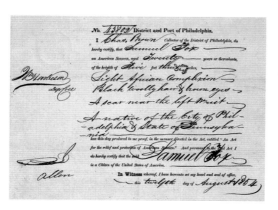

Frederick Douglass escaped to freedom carrying a borrowed seaman's papers, like the one shown here.

Getting his bearings on the busy streets of New York, he saw a black man whom he had known in Maryland as Jake. The man now called himself William Dixon. Dixon warned the newcomer to beware, and Frederick took care to "trust no man with my secret." There were black men roaming the city who would inform on their fellow men to slave catchers for only a few dollars. Also, he warned Frederick to avoid rooming at boarding houses where black people stayed, or to seek work on the docks, for these were places where escapees were commonly captured.

Frederick and Anna Wed

Before he left Maryland, Frederick was given the address of David Ruggles, a black man who lived in New York. Ruggles was an important member of an organization that protected runaway slaves. He also helped slaves escape to safety in states farther north or in Canada. From Ruggles's home, Frederick wrote to Anna and asked her to join him. The couple married when Anna arrived in the city.

Frederick and Anna Douglass's marriage license shows Frederick identified as Frederick Johnson.

To avoid being identified and caught, Frederick used the last name of "Johnson" for the marriage license. It read that a marriage between Frederick Johnson and Anna Murray had taken place on September 15, 1838. For her wedding, Anna wore a new plum-colored silk dress, and Frederick was dressed in a new suit. New York was a large city in a non-slave, northern state. Yet, Frederick and Anna felt unsafe from the slave catchers who roamed the streets. It was not unusual for them to come upon posters offering rewards for the recapture of runaway slaves.

Yet, Frederick and Anna felt unsafe from the slave catchers who roamed the streets.

Mr. Ruggles suggested that Frederick and his wife might have a better chance at starting a new life in New Bedford, Massachusetts. He had friends who ran a small business there. The town was a seaport, where Frederick could find work using his skills as a ship's caulker. Another advantage was that New Bedford was a center of the abolitionist movement.

Abolitionists wanted to end slavery in America. Both black and white residents in New Bedford were actively determined to keep slave catchers away. When a free black man there had threatened to inform on a fugitive slave for money, members of a black church turned on the informer and threatened him with his life if he did not leave town.

A common sight in many large cities, north and south, were posters that offered rewards of $100 to $300 or more for the capture of fugitive slaves. Such posters gave the slave's name and described the runaway's skin color, height, and other features, such as scars from beatings or from having smallpox. There were often details about the clothes the person might have been wearing at the time he or she fled. One poster described a seventeen-year-old girl named Emily who took with her "one dark calico and one blue-and-white dress, a red bonnet, a white striped shawl, and [a pair of] slippers."

Some posters were created to alert both free blacks and fugitive slaves to be watchful. One dated April 24, 1831, gave the following warning, in part: "Caution! Colored People of Boston, one and all, you are hereby respectfully cautioned and advised, to avoid conversing with the watchmen and police officers of Boston. For since the recent order of the Mayor and Aldermen, they [watchmen and police officers] are empowered to act as kidnappers and slave catchers."

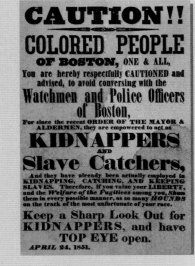

This handbill warns black people, both fugitive and free, of slave catchers. It was printed after a runaway slave was captured in Boston following the Fugitive Slave Act.

CHAPTER 6

A New Name in New Bedford

I had no master who could take it [earned money] from me—that it was mine—that my hands were my own.

Arriving in New Bedford, Frederick and Anna found the home of Mary and Nathan Johnson, a wealthy, middle-aged, African American couple. They lived in a neat, large frame house that had a front yard blooming with flowers. One side of the house was used for their catering business. The Johnsons offered a room in their home to Frederick and Anna until the couple could get settled.

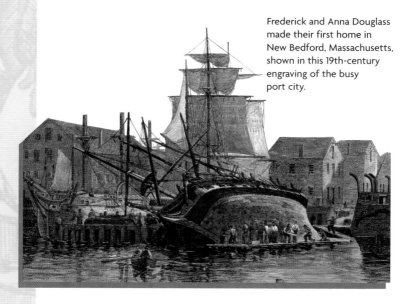

Frederick and Anna Douglass made their first home in New Bedford, Massachusetts, shown in this 19th-century engraving of the busy port city.

Frederick was impressed with Nathan Johnson, who kept a small library of books. One morning, Nathan commented that "Johnson" was a name often used by blacks who had moved north. In fact, there were so many Johnson families in the town, that at times it was hard to distinguish one family from another. Knowing Frederick's love of books and literature, Nathan proposed that his guests take the name *Douglas* after a character in Walter Scott's book, *Lady of the Lake*. Frederick liked the name, but he added an extra *s* at the end. From then on, he was known as Frederick Douglass.

From then on, he was known as Frederick Douglass.

On his strolls around New Bedford, he discovered that the white people in this town were wealthy, but had no slaves. They lived in houses that were elegantly furnished and had modern conveniences and comforts. This also held true for many of the black people who lived there, including his hosts, the Johnsons. Coming from a slave state, Frederick had been brought up to believe that only poor and ignorant people had no slaves.

During his job search at the town's docks, Frederick Douglass was even more amazed by the workers who went about their jobs quietly. There was none of the loud shouting, cursing, chanting, or singing of sad songs that he had heard from the slave gangs who worked on Baltimore's waterfront. Nor did he hear the crack of the whip used to control the workers.

However, for all of New Bedford's promise, and despite his shipbuilding experience in Baltimore, Frederick had difficulty finding employment. When one shipbuilder hired him to work as a caulker, the white workers threatened to leave their jobs and their unfinished work until Fredrick was let go. While the practice of slavery was forbidden, Douglass found that many white people in town were racially **prejudiced** against its black citizens. He saw that black children and white children attended the same schools and sat side by side, but blacks attending white churches had to sit in separate sections.

In the winter of 1838, a few months after their arrival in New Bedford, the Douglasses learned that Anna was expecting their first child. The couple rented two rooms for nine dollars a month. Frederick had found work as a day laborer. He sawed wood, shoveled coal, dug cellars, and loaded and unloaded ships. On his first job, he hauled in coal for a Unitarian minister who gave him two half-dollars. Clasping the coins in his hand, he thought, "I had no master who could take it from me—that it was mine— that my hands were my own." Although he could not be hired for his trade as a caulker, he found work to support his growing family. The Douglasses' first child, Rosetta, was born in June 1839. Their first son, Lewis Henry was born sixteen months later.

The first child born to Frederick and Anna Douglass was Rosetta Douglass, shown as a young adult in this photograph.

A Soul Set on Fire

One day, Douglass met a young man on the street who gave him a trial subscription to *The Liberator*, a newspaper edited by abolitionist William Lloyd Garrison, a white man and a leader of the American Anti-Slavery Society. Garrison and his newspaper were dedicated to ending slavery. Douglass was so excited about what he read in the paper that he kept it on a table next to his Bible. He later wrote that "The paper became my meat and drink—My soul was set all on fire."

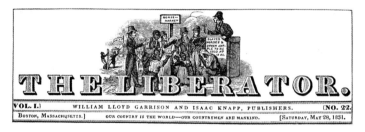

The May 28, 1831, masthead of William Lloyd Garrison's *The Liberator* states "Our Country is the World—Our Countrymen Are Mankind."

Frederick and Anna joined the New Bedford Zion Methodist Church. The couple soon participated in the church's small black congregation and in New Bedford's black community. They were especially pleased with Thomas James, Zion's new minister, a former slave who was active in the antislavery movement. Douglass became a popular Sunday school teacher, and Reverend James made Frederick a lay preacher who would occasionally deliver sermons, usually on the evils of slavery. Having visited several black churches, Frederick noticed that the subject of slavery was rarely discussed.

Another topic of concern to him was an article that he had read in *The Liberator*. There was a proposal that was supported by groups of whites and even some blacks to relocate free blacks

A Black Colony

Most free blacks and whites who supported the rights of black people, felt that former slaves should be allowed to become American citizens. Yet, some politicians, such as Thomas Jefferson, and other white citizens, felt that they could not truly adjust to living with whites in America. There were also black leaders who believed that they would never be free of discrimination in the United States. Perhaps they would lead better lives in a colony in Africa.

In 1816, Paul Cuffee, a wealthy shipowner and a **Quaker** of African American and Native American heritage, sailed to the British colony of Sierra Leone in Africa. Thirty-eight free black people sailed with him to begin a settlement named Freetown. Cuffee had the support of the British and United States governments and planned to carry African Americans to a new homeland once a year. In return, he would sail back to America with valuable African resources, such as timber for building and metal ores. Cuffee died suddenly in 1817,

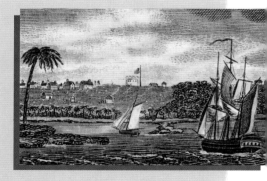

An 1832 colored engraving shows the settlement of Monrovia, Liberia, where freed slaves from the United States arrived to form a new colony in Africa.

but the American Colonization Society (ACS) was formed that year to continue his plans. In 1847, the colony became the independent nation of Liberia, and by 1867, the ACS had sent more than 13,000 free blacks to the colony.

from America to a colony in Africa. This plan was seen as a solution to "the problem" of what to do with former slaves.

The proposal to send blacks to Africa was an outrage to Douglass. He was one of many blacks who saw it as a trick to weaken the opposition to slavery. In one of his Sunday sermons on the subject, he said that the United

The proposal to send blacks to Africa was an outrage to Douglass.

States was as much the true home of black people as it was for anyone in this country. African Americans had helped build America, which also profited from their labors. He sent his comments to *The Liberator*. To his delight, they were published in the March 1839 issue.

After living in New Bedford for several months, the Douglasses found steady jobs. Once again, Anna found work as a servant. In addition to his work as a laborer, Frederick was also hired to do odd jobs at different factories—one that made whale oil and another that produced brass items. Eventually, the couple earned enough money to leave their rented apartment and move into a small house.

With whatever free time Frederick had, he also attended lectures at American Anti-Slavery Society meetings. At a meeting in April 1839, the invited speaker was William Lloyd Garrison, editor of *The Liberator*. Balding and with glasses perched on his nose, Garrison's mild-mannered appearance gave no hint that his emotionally-charged speeeches on the immorality of owning slaves would stir audiences in lecture halls throughout New England. Douglass was greatly impressed by Garrison who, through his writings in *The Liberator*, had become his hero. By the end of the evening, Frederick knew that he, too, would be an orator. He too could speak about the cruelty of slavery because he had been one.

William Lloyd Garrison (1805–1879)

This is an 1860 oil-painted daguerreotype of William Lloyd Garrison, one of America's most important abolitionists and an early mentor of Frederick Douglass.

When William Lloyd Garrison was born in Newburyport, Massachusetts, in 1805, slavery had been abolished in the state for more than twenty years. He had encountered few black people growing up in his small town. Yet, he emerged as the leading voice among white abolitionists in the nineteenth century. Garrison founded *The Liberator*, his newspaper in which his editorials proclaimed that slavery was morally wrong. He was also an important leader in the American Anti-Slavery Society.

Garrison had little faith in overturning slavery through political or legislative means. He believed in educating people about the injustice of slavery through *The Liberator* and through his lectures given at Anti-Slavery Society meetings. It was his view that abolitionists should demand an immediate end to slavery.

Garrison also held very strong positions on several other issues: For example, it was his belief that abolitionists should refuse to vote or run for office and that the United States Constitution, which considered blacks as only three-fifths of a person, discriminated in its treatment of black people. He also argued that non-slave-holding states in the North should split from the South, which held millions of blacks in enslavement. This separation would create a nation free of slave-holding states. At the same time, Garrison was strongly against violence in any attempts to free slaves.

In the spring of 1841, William C. Coffin, a wealthy abolitionist and Quaker, attended an antislavery meeting at Douglass's church. After hearing Frederick speak of his experiences as a slave, Coffin invited Frederick to attend a convention of the Massachusetts Anti-Slavery Society during the summer.

The Society's meeting was to be held thirty miles from the coast of Massachusetts on the island of Nantucket. In August, Frederick attended the Anti-Slavery Society meeting without Anna and their children. His saw this trip as a small personal holiday and an opportunity to become more active in the abolitionist movement.

A Powerful New Voice

Word-of-mouth news, perhaps started by William C. Coffin, had reached the residents of the town of Nantucket that a black man—and former slave—would address the Massachusetts

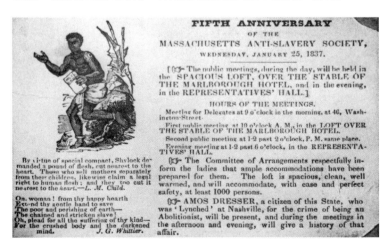

A Massachusetts Anti-Slavery Society announcement also featured speaker Amos Dresser, a white abolitionist who was publicly whipped in Nashville, Tennessee, for being a member of an anti-slavery organization.

Anti-Slavery Society meeting that month. Many of the residents of this wealthy seaport were Quakers who long supported the cause of abolition. There was concern that the hall, which usually held music and arts events, could not hold the crowds that promised to attend the meeting. Instead, the meeting was moved to a large structure at the end of town called the Big Shop, which was owned by the Coffin family and was used for building great whaling boats.

Determined to see and hear Douglass speak, people crowded into the Big Shop. All of the seats were taken, and any standing room filled up immediately. Boys and young men climbed the rafters overhead. Those unable to make it into the building looked in through the opened windows. Many of them were from the New Guinea section of Nantucket, which was a black community.

William Lloyd Garrison opened the meeting with a resolution, which was a statement that was directed not only toward the wickedness of southern slave owners, but toward the prejudice that many Northerners held toward nonwhites, as well. He warned the gathering about the "cruel injustice against those whose skins are not colored like our own." Many speakers who were important leaders in the antislavery movement followed with speeches of their own to second Garrison's resolution.

The audience saw a tall, handsome, brown-skinned man with a full mane of hair stand before them.

Then Garrison turned to Douglass and invited him to rise and have his say. The audience saw a tall, handsome, brown-skinned man with a full mane of hair stand before them. Stammering out his first words, Frederick spoke in a low voice until the audience urged him to speak up. Gaining courage,

Douglass began to tell the story of his life, starting with his years as a child slave and ending with his journey to freedom. He dramatically described and acted out the characters that had played a role in his life, both good and bad.

The audience was captivated by Frederick's heartfelt story. When he finished speaking, they applauded and cheered loudly. William Garrison quickly took the stage and, pointing to Frederick, asked if they had been listening to "a thing . . . or a man?" The audience responded, "A man! A man!" When Garrison asked if this man should be sent back to

The audience was captivated by Frederick's heartfelt story.

slavery, the entire room rose and shouted, "No! No! No!" As Frederick stood surrounded by hundreds of supporters, the antislavery movement had found a powerful new voice. Douglass was so carried away by his own speech that he later said he did not remember a single sentence of it.

Several leaders of the Massachusetts Anti-Slavery Society came forward to shake Frederick's hand. They invited Douglass to become a paid speaker for the society, which meant traveling to other cities with its members and speaking at abolitionist meetings. Like other lecturers of the society, he would also be expected to sell subscriptions of *The Liberator* to people who attended the meetings. Douglass agreed to the offer immediately. He strongly believed in the mission of the society, and the job was also a great opportunity to be employed with a regular salary.

When Frederick returned to New Bedford, neither he nor Anna could have guessed how his new career would change their lives. It would carry him away from the simple, domestic life that they had shared before his trip to Nantucket. Anna was unable to leave or take their small children and travel with him. Frederick would have to travel weeks at a time without his family. The money Frederick earned from his speaking engagements, plus the financial help he received from the Anti-Slavery Society, enabled him to buy a house for his family in Lynn, Massachusetts.

An Abolitionist Onstage

For two years, Douglass spoke at antislavery meetings in towns and cities throughout New England. Despite his popularity on the lecture stage, not all went well during his travels. At times, Douglass encountered humiliating incidents of racism. These experiences reminded him that he was a black man in a country in which black people were still considered to be unequal—whether they were free or not.

Black train travelers during the 19th century who would sit in first-class seats were angrily removed to less-comfortable cars reserved for blacks.

During his travels by train, he was almost always forced to leave his seat in the first-class car and move to the "Negro" car. Frederick strongly objected when this occurred. Sometimes he had to be dragged out of his seat and tossed around before he left the car. On one occasion, when he asked a conductor to explain why he should leave his first-class seat, the conductor called for help to remove him. Douglass was determined to hold on to the seat, and he did, even when the trainmen threw him and the seat onto a station platform.

He would later write that, "Prejudice against color is stronger north than south. It hangs around my neck like a heavy weight." At times, this prejudice was more of a danger than a heavy weight.

An Angry Mob

On a six-month tour of what were considered the "western" states of America, Frederick and other society speakers came face-to-face with people who hated abolitionists and their message. At a meeting in Pendleton, Indiana, a drunken mob of white men heckled Douglass by making fun of him and two other abolitionists at a lecture hall. After the hecklers surrounded the stage and threw rotten eggs at the speakers' faces, they dared Douglass and his associates to a fight. Trying to protect his friends, Douglass grabbed a wooden board and went after the attackers. Seeing a black man attacking white men made the mob turn on Frederick and shout, "Kill him!" One man used a club to break Douglass's right hand. His colleagues were injured as well, but they all managed to escape.

Despite these rare outbursts, Douglass was in such demand that wherever he traveled he was able to draw large crowds who were favorable to his message. The American Anti-Slavery Society selected him to tour New York and other eastern states with important abolitionist leaders such as William Lloyd Garrison and Wendell Philips, another famous orator.

Douglass's deep, rich voice swayed the audiences with his stories. His early lectures dealt with his experiences as an enslaved child and young man. He not only told of his own beatings, but of those given to women, to elderly people, and to young children, as well. Then, changing the mood from these tragic stories, he could have audiences laughing while acting out a humorous version of his fight with Covey, the slave breaker.

Doubting His Story

Not everyone was comfortable with Douglass's confident manner and elegant use of language. Some people commented that he didn't talk like a slave, look like a slave, or act like a slave. People doubted that only six years before, he had been a slave who had never gone to school. At one lecture, he actually heard a member of the audience whisper, "He's never been a slave, I'll warrant ye!"

Some people commented that he didn't talk like a slave, look like a slave, or act like a slave.

Douglass always took great care in his speeches to avoid giving his former name, the real name of his owner, the state where he had been enslaved, and other details that could identify him. He was, after all, still the property of Thomas Auld of St. Michaels, Maryland. This information would not only endanger his freedom, but could be harmful for anyone who had helped him.

Some people said: "He don't tell us where he come from— what his [owner's] name was—or how he got away . . . ." Members of the Society suggested that perhaps Douglass might keep "a little of the plantation" in his speeches. Many people of that time, whether they would admit it or not, expected a former slave to speak and to present himself as an uneducated person. Douglass, who had gone to great lengths to educate himself and to carry himself with pride, was insulted by the suggestion and chose to ignore it.

Still, he grew concerned that people did not believe him, and he worried that he might be seen as an imposter. In 1845, as more people questioned the truthfulness behind his speeches, Douglass decided to write an autobiography of his life. In his book, he used the real names of people, places, and events as he recalled them. He began writing of his wretched childhood and included events through his escape to freedom in the North. The title of his book was the *Narrative of the Life of Frederick Douglass, an American Slave, Written by Himself.*

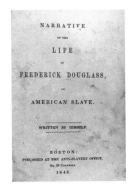

An original cover of *Narrative of the Life of Frederick Douglass an American Slave, Written by Himself*. Since 1845, millions of copies of this book have been sold.

Before he published his book, he had abolitionist lawyer Wendell Phillips read it. Phillips was impressed with the book, but he was concerned for Douglass's safety and wrote, ". . . there is no single spot—however narrow or desolate—where a fugitive can plant himself and say, 'I am safe.'" He wrote that if he were in Frederick's place, he would throw the book into the fireplace. Douglass was not discouraged, and the *Narrative* was published in May 1845. Each copy was sold for fifty cents. By the fall of that year, more than 4,500 copies were sold in the United States. The story of a runaway slave's passion, courage, and triumph had people eager to read about it. The book became a bestseller. Within five years, more than 30,000 copies of Douglass's *Narrative* were sold in the United States and in Europe.

The *Narrative* enabled Douglass to reach a wider audience on the cause of destroying slavery. At the same time, the book also threatened his freedom. He was still an escaped slave, and by federal law, Frederick Douglass—once known as Frederick Bailey—could be legally returned to his owner, Thomas Auld. Sensing this danger, in the summer of 1845, Douglass made another great escape. But it was not as daring as the one he had made to run from slavery in Maryland.

CHAPTER 7

Freedom Bought in Great Britain

I long to see a face which I have seen in America.

On August 16, 1845, Frederick Douglass boarded the *Cambria*, a British steamship bound for Great Britain. Through friends in the American Anti-Slavery Society, he left with a fully scheduled lecture tour of the British Isles. Abolitionists in Ireland, Scotland, and England, where slavery had been abolished in 1833, looked forward to hearing this famous American black man. For his part, Frederick had long wanted to travel to Europe, though his voyage across the Atlantic was not all smooth sailing. He was irritated to be denied a first-class cabin. Instead, he was assigned to travel in the below decks steerage, or second-class, section of the boat. On board, Douglass was an object of both admiration and curiosity. He was invited to visit fellow passengers in their first-class cabins. A family of famous musicians went below to his second-class quarters and sang "their sweetest songs" in what he called his "rude deck."

During his tour of Great Britain, Douglass's family remained in Lynn, Massachusetts. At home were Anna Douglass and their four children: six-year-old Rosetta, five-year-old Lewis, three-year-old Frederick, and ten-month-old Charles. A woman known as "Aunt Harriet," who may have been a relative of Frederick's, had also become a member of the household.

After years of Frederick's long absences, Anna had become accustomed to raising her family alone. The family lived comfortably. Sales from his *Narrative* autobiography helped to support them, and Anna brought in extra income by sewing shoes in her home for a shoe manufacturer.

On the other side of the Atlantic Ocean, Douglass thrived in his new environment. His speaking tour through Ireland, Scotland, and England was most successful. He was greeted with great enthusiasm wherever he went. William Lloyd Garrison joined Douglass in a lecture tour of Great Britain in the summer of 1846. By that time, some of his new acquaintances encouraged him to consider moving to England. They tried to convince Douglass that he would not face the kind of racial prejudice found in the States.

In this colored woodcut, Frederick Douglass is shown lecturing to a receptive audience in Great Britain, where he lived for 21 months.

Thinking of a Move

The idea of living in Great Britain appealed to Douglass briefly, and he wrote to his family about the idea of moving abroad. He also wrote to other black friends in America, inviting them to also relocate. He had become a famous person throughout Britain, but he was homesick. He wrote a letter to an associate back in the United States that contained the sentence "I long to see a face which I have seen in America."

He also wondered if moving his family to England would be a wise decision. Frederick realized that Anna and the children might never feel at home in a foreign country. Despite his successful lecture tour, he missed his family, but he also had another nagging concern: Was it safe to return to his homeland where he was still a "wanted man"? In March 1846, Frederick learned that Thomas Auld had sold his ownership of Douglass to his brother, Hugh Auld, in Baltimore for one hundred dollars.

Douglass's travels took him to the town of Newcastle-upon-Tyne in England, where he met the Richardsons, a family of Quakers. Ellen Richardson was the headmistress of a girls' school; her brother and sister-in-law, Henry and Anna Richardson, were all active in Britain's antislavery movement. Douglass developed a strong friendship with the Richardsons. After he had spent some time with them, they became aware that Frederick was torn between his desire to move his family to England, which may not have been practical, and his longing to return to the United States, where he was a wanted man.

He had become a famous person throughout Britain, but he was homesick.

Buying Freedom

It seemed the only solution to Frederick's dilemma was to buy his freedom. Ellen Richardson's brother, Henry, contacted a fellow lawyer in Baltimore to act on Frederick's behalf to request what the Aulds would consider a fair price for their slave. The agreed price was £150—the English currency for U.S. dollars—which was equivalent to about $700 in 1846. Ellen raised the money to help buy Frederick's freedom, and shortly thereafter, on December 12, 1846, manumission papers to free Douglass were legally signed. Frederick Douglass was now a free black man!

That December, Frederick spent Christmas with the Richardsons, where he met Julia Griffiths, a woman who would later play a major role in his life. Julia, an abolitionist and an intelligent woman, had followed Frederick's writings. When Frederick returned to the United States, she was one of the first people with whom he shared his plans to publish an antislavery newspaper.

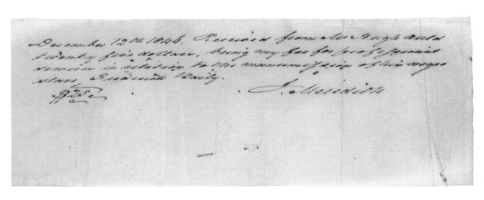

A photograph of Frederick Douglass's manumission papers, which were signed on December 12, 1846.

Douglass sailed back to the United States and arrived in Boston on April 20, 1847. He received a warm homecoming from Anna and his children and lost little time working on plans to establish his own newspaper. He had received about £500 from his friends in England and Ireland, who raised the money to help with the expenses of his new project.

First, however, Frederick had made a promise to William Lloyd Garrison that he would join him on a lecture tour through Massachusetts, New York, Pennsylvania, and Ohio. At the end of the tour, he announced the plans for his newspaper to Garrison and other members of the American Anti-Slavery Society. The proposal did not sit well with Garrison and the Society members. They feared that Douglass's paper would compete with *The Liberator*, especially among black readers. Although their friendship was not as close as it had been in the past, Garrison wished Douglass and his paper good luck.

Frederick also revealed that he would move his family from Lynn, Massachusetts, to Rochester, New York. During his lecture visits to Rochester, Frederick was drawn to the city because of the many abolitionists who lived there. Some of the antislavery organizations in Rochester were led by women prominent in the fight for women's rights, which Douglass also supported.

Some of the antislavery organizations in Rochester were led by women prominent in the fight for women's rights, which Douglass also supported.

Black Newspapers

In 1827, John B. Russwurm, one of the first free African American men to graduate from college, and another free black man Samuel E. Cornish, published *Freedom's Journal*. The journal was published twenty years before Douglass started his newspaper the *North Star*. Black-owned and edited newspapers were important institutions in the African American community. By 1862, there were more than forty newspapers published in the United States by African Americans. They offered a point of view that was not found in white-owned newspapers. For instance, African American Willis Hodges started *The Ram's Horn* in New York City in 1847 after a white-owned newspaper refused to print his opinions. The newspaper had run articles proposing that blacks be denied the right to vote. Instead of printing Hodge's angry reply to the editor, the newspaper made him pay fifteen dollars to have his comments printed, then ran his reply as an advertisement. Hodges started *The Ram's Horn* so that the views of black readers would be featured.

John B. Russwurm, one of the first black people to graduate from an American college, helped publish *Freedom's Journal* in 1827—one the many black newspapers of that era.

Black newspapers kept black communities up to date on local and national politics. They were also a source of uplifting stories about the achievements of African Americans.

CHAPTER 8

The *North Star*

Right is of no sex—Truth is of no color—God is the Father of us all, and we are all Bretheren.

In the fall of 1847, Douglass traveled to Rochester in western New York State with the intention of getting his paper off the ground. He had £500 (roughly U.S. $1,000) from investors in Great Britain, and he was given additional funds from another friend in England to purchase a printing press. He also received contributions when he needed them from Gerrit Smith, a wealthy New York State landowner and abolitionist. Douglass named his paper the *North Star* after the *Northern Star*, a newspaper published by English rights activist Feargus O'Connor.

The front page of Douglass's *North Star*, June 2, 1848, issue featured a variety of articles of interest to its readers.

Douglass published the first issue of the *North Star* on December 3, 1847. The four-page paper came out once a week; the price of subscription was two dollars a year. Douglass's motto on the masthead read: "Right is of no sex—Truth is of no color—God is the Father of us all, and we are all Bretheren." Copies of the paper were sent to Douglass's friends around the country and to his supporters in Canada, Mexico, Great Britain, and even in Australia.

The *North Star* received great praise in its early days, but it had a slow start financially. Subscriptions trickled in and the expense of running the paper forced Douglass to return to the lecture circuit. His two older sons, Lewis and Frederick, helped cut costs by learning to work for the *North Star* as printer's apprentices. To keep the paper in business and cover its expenses, Douglass had to acquire a loan pledge on his house.

Eventually, the *North Star* became the best-known black newspaper in the United States and was noted for publishing the goals and achievements of black people around the country. It also enabled Douglass to meet more fellow black abolitionists. The

> *Eventually, the North Star became the best-known black newspaper in the United States . . .*

publication was an important arena in which black leaders and writers could discuss their opinions about the issues facing African America people.

An Advocate for Women's Rights

With the *North Star* launched, Frederick moved Anna and three of their four children to Rochester. Frederick had sent Rosetta, their oldest daughter, to nearby Albany, New York, to live and study at the home of abolitionist sisters Abigail and

In 1848, Douglass moved his family to Rochester, New York, which is pictured in this 1840 street scene engraving.

Lydia Mott—cousins of women's rights activist Lucretia Coffin Mott. In April 1848, the Douglass family bought a two-story, nine-room brick house on Rochester's Alexander Street, where a year later, Annie, their fifth child, was born.

Anna had been reluctant to move—once again. She had willingly settled into their first home in the New Bedford community and had made friends at the church where Frederick served as a preacher. During their years in Lynn, Anna devoted her life to her children, and she was proud of her home and the garden that she had kept for years. While the move to Rochester meant an exciting career opportunity for Frederick, for Anna, a homebody who did not share his world of travel experiences and did not know many of his associates, the move meant dealing with the loneliness of starting over in yet another city. In the words of her daughter Rosetta, the heroism of Frederick Douglass "was a story made possible by the unswerving loyalty of Anna Murray."

Women in the abolitionist movement had long been Douglass's allies just as he had been an advocate for women's rights. Frederick was often in contact with educated women who were well-read and well-traveled. He was proud that Anna was a good mother who had taught their children to have good manners and to be hard-working individuals. Still, he was pained that Anna was illiterate. Frederick hired a tutor to teach her to read and write, but despite these efforts, she remained illiterate, and she showed little interest in politics or the antislavery movement.

Frederick was often in contact with educated women who were well-read and well-traveled.

Anna's status was not unlike many women of that time, black or white. In the late 1840s, American women were expected to marry, raise their children, and keep their husband's house. Married women were not permitted to own property, and their husbands dealt with the world on their behalf. Women could not vote, hold political office, or even speak in public before mixed audiences of men and women or blacks and whites. While women in the abolitionist movement actively worked for the rights of enslaved blacks, they were not entitled to many of the same privileges that blacks were fighting for.

There were growing numbers of women who were working to change the status of women. Frederick Douglass sympathized with them and took an active part in their efforts. In July 1848, Douglass spoke at the first Women's Rights Convention in Seneca Falls, New York. Taking on critics of the event, he wrote an editorial in the *North Star*, saying that people would rather discuss the rights of animals than discuss the rights of women.

The Seneca Falls Convention

Among the organizers of the first Women's Rights Convention were Elizabeth Cady Stanton, the wife of an anti-slavery activist, and Lucretia Coffin Mott, a Quaker preacher. The focus of the meeting was to discuss the social, civil, and religious rights of women.

The two-day meeting was held on July 19 and 20, 1848, at the Wesleyan Methodist Church in Seneca Falls. A Declaration of Sentiments, written by Elizabeth Cady Stanton, was based on the Declaration of Independence and was the focus of the meeting. Three hundred women plus forty men crowded into the church for the convention. All of the resolutions in the Declaration of Sentiments were passed, except for the one demanding the women's right to vote. The Seneca Falls Convention was the first public discussion of this issue in the United States. For days following the convention, newspaper editorials and church sermons criticized the event and the idea that women demanded the right to vote.

Abolitionist Elizabeth Cady Stanton fought both for the rights of women and African Americans. She is shown here addressing the Seneca Falls Women's Rights Convention in 1848.

A Great Scandal

With the help of his friend Julia Griffiths, who arrived from England in 1849, Douglass was able to turn the newspaper into a profitable enterprise. Not only had Griffiths raised the money to start the paper, she also had the business sense to keep the paper operating. Julia applied her writing and editorial skills to the *North Star* and to managing Frederick's speaking schedule. She and Frederick were often seen walking arm-in-arm through the streets of Rochester, deep in discussion. In the nineteenth century, this strange friendship between a black man and a white woman caused a great **scandal** in Rochester.

Members of the abolitionist community frowned on Douglass's relationship with Julia, too. Some said that she hurt the antislavery cause. Despite the criticism, Douglass defended Griffiths and even invited her to move into the Douglass household as a tutor. Frederick thought that Julia could help the children with their lessons. Anna, however, was very uncomfortable about Julia's presence in her home. Even though Julia knew that she was a source of humiliation for Frederick's family, she lived in the Douglass home for three years until 1852. That year, Julia moved in with other friends and stayed for three more years before returning to England in 1855.

Douglass and Griffiths remained friends and wrote letters to each other until his death. He always remained grateful for her assistance and the support that she gave to the *North Star*. There had been many whispers about the relationship between Douglass and Griffiths, but there was never any evidence of improper behavior between the two.

CHAPTER 9

A Country in Turmoil

The Fourth of July is yours, not mine. You may rejoice, I must mourn . . . .

Frederick Douglass had become the most famous champion of the antislavery movement in the United States, but some abolitionists resented that he was often the focus of attention. Meetings of the Anti-Slavery Society speakers would be interrupted with shouts demanding for "Douglass! Douglass!" to step up to the stage. During their years of working together, Frederick and William Lloyd Garrison had developed a strong friendship and respect for each other. But by the early 1850s, Douglass's increasing popularity and their widening differences of opinion on how to abolish slavery broke that bond between them.

John Brown was a radical abolitionist who planned and carried out a failed slave rebellion at Harpers Ferry, Virginia.

Garrison believed that educating slaveholders and the public about the evils of slavery, and thus putting an end to it, was the morally right thing to do. Failing that, he argued that states in the North should split from the South to create a nation free of slaveholding states. He opposed violence as a means of achieving this goal. Unlike Garrison, Douglass was not entirely convinced the South would end the system of slavery peacefully. In 1847, Douglass had met with John Brown, a revolutionary abolitionist. Brown hoped to start a rebellion among slaves in the South. While Douglass didn't agree with John Brown's plot—which he felt would bring violence—he was concerned that slavery would not end without bloodshed.

In 1848, Douglass attended a convention of the Free-Soil Party. The party opposed admitting new slave states into the Union. Douglass was persuaded that this political action could stop the spread of slavery in the territories and new states west of the Mississippi River. At the eighteenth annual meeting of the American Anti-Slavery Society in 1851, Douglass stood before its members and, disputing Garrison's beliefs, stated that the Constitution, which promoted "liberty for all," was an antislavery document. He further announced that he intended to encourage readers of the *North Star* to become politically active. He wanted people to pressure political lawmakers and candidates running for office to reveal their stand on slavery-related issues.

He further announced that he intended to encourage readers of the North Star to become politically active.

Douglass's comments angered Garrison, who believed that participation in politics was not the way to end slavery. This announcement by Douglass was the final blow to their friendship. For the rest of their lives, the two men continued to fight for equality but each in his own way. To further claim his independence, Douglass changed the name of the *North Star* to *Frederick Douglass' Paper* in 1851. The paper eventually became

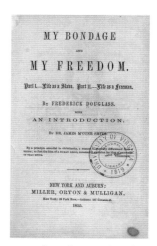

MY BONDAGE

AND

MY FREEDOM.

Part I.—Life as a Slave. Part II.—Life as a Freeman.

By FREDERICK DOUGLASS.

WITH

AN INTRODUCTION.

By DR. JAMES M'CUNE SMITH.

By a principle essential to christianity, a person is eternally differenced from a
thing; so that the idea of a HUMAN BEING, necessarily excludes the idea of property
in that being.

NEW YORK AND AUBURN:
MILLER, ORTON & MULLIGAN.
New York: 25 Park Row.—Auburn: 107 Genesee st.
1855.

My Bondage and My Freedom was Douglas's second successful autobiography, which was published in 1855 and sold 15,000 copies in two months.

a monthly newspaper called *Douglass' Monthly* although, nine years later, Douglass stopped publishing his paper all together.

In the summer of 1852, Douglass bought and moved his family to a farmhouse on a hill located about two miles outside the city of Rochester, but he kept the house on Alexander Street as an **investment**. Douglass also wrote and published his second book, *My Bondage and My Freedom,* in 1855. The book is said to be Douglass's declaration of independence as a free man.

Douglass's Fifth of July Speech

That same year, the Rochester Ladies' Anti-Slavery Society invited Douglass to share his views on what the Fourth of July holiday meant to him. He agreed but requested that he be permitted to deliver the speech on the Fifth of July.

Douglass then spent two weeks in late June writing a speech about Independence Day. On July 5, 1852, he spoke in front of a packed audience in Rochester's Corinthian Hall. In his deep baritone voice, he began with words of praise for the founders of the United States of America and for the American Revolution.

Douglass changed his theme in the middle of the speech, saying the day was not a day of holiday for black people. It was not a celebration for those enslaved in the South, nor was it a true holiday for free black people who lived in the North.

This 1855 portrait of Frederick Douglass is a daguerrotype, which was an early form of photography.

Explaining to his audience of mostly white abolitionists, "The Fourth of July is yours, not mine," he said. "You may rejoice, I must mourn. . . .

"What, to the American slave, is your Fourth of July? I answer: a day that reveals to him, more than all other days of the year, the gross injustice and cruelty to which he is the constant victim." At the end of the speech, his audience rose to applaud him. Many people believe that this speech was the most powerful antislavery speech given by Douglass or by any other abolitionist orator.

Blows to the Movement

By the 1850s, a great divide about admitting new states to the Union was taking place in Congress between legislators from the North and the South. Which states could be "free" and which states could be "slave" states became a troublesome issue. Until 1819, an equal number of free and slave states made up the union that became the United States. When settlers in Missouri asked to be admitted to the Union as a slave state, it would have upset that balance and given the South more political power.

Then, in 1820, Congress made a **compromise**. It admitted Missouri as a slave state, and gave statehood to Maine, as a free state. This action was known as the Missouri Compromise. At the same time, Congress also created an imaginary line through western territories that had not yet become states. Slavery was forbidden in new states admitted above that line; states admitted below that line would permit slavery.

But when California declared itself a free state in 1849 and wanted to be admitted into the Union, southern states vowed to leave. To maintain the balance between free and slave states and to calm southern threats, Congress passed a series of laws, including passage of the Fugitive Slave Act—the most damaging piece of legislation to affect the well being of blacks everywhere in the United States. California was then admitted into the Union as a free state on September 9, 1850. Although this agreement became known as the Compromise of 1850, for black people, there was no compromise—only misery.

The Fugitive Slave Act appointed federal commissioners to assist in recapturing fugitive slaves, who were routinely denied jury trials where they could testify on their own behalf to become free. Instead, they were sent back to their owners. The law not only endangered fugitive slaves but also free blacks who had the

A MAN KIDNAPPED!

A PUBLIC MEETING AT

FANEUIL HALL!

WILL BE HELD

THIS FRIDAY EVEN'G,

May 26th, at 7 o'clock,

To secure justice for A MAN CLAIMED AS A SLAVE by a

VIRGINIA KIDNAPPER!

And NOW IMPRISONED IN BOSTON COURT HOUSE, in defiance of the Laws of Massachusetts. Shall he be plunged into the Hell of Virginia Slavery by a Massachusetts Judge of Probate?

BOSTON, May 26th, 1854.

Many blacks—both fugitives and free—were kidnapped because of the Fugitive Slave Act. This poster announces the kidnapping and trial of a fugitive slave who was returned to his owner in Virginia.

misfortune of being captured. Even if they were carrying manumission papers, they could be sold to plantation owners in the South who sometimes produced false documents to prove ownership. Anyone assisting a fugitive slave could be fined as much as $1,000 and put into jail.

Frederick Douglass and other abolitionists opposed this law and bitterly spoke against it. They wrote newspaper articles, had public demonstrations, and encouraged people to defy it. Douglass was outraged that the oaths of any two villains were sufficient to confine a free man to slavery for life.

Another blow against the antislavery movement occurred a few years after the Compromise of 1850. In 1857, the U.S. Supreme Court wrote a decision that declared slaves were not citizens of the United States and were the personal properties of their slave owners. The decision was based on a suit brought by a slave named Dred Scott, and it outraged Douglass.

The Dred Scott Decision

Dred Scott was an illiterate slave living in Missouri in 1846 when he appealed to the St. Louis Circuit Court to be granted his freedom. He argued that he had lived with and worked for his owner—an army surgeon—for a period of time in Illinois, which was a free state. Back then, under Missouri law, any slave who lived on free soil, even for a short time, could be declared free.

A number of delays prevented Scott's case from being heard until January 1850. A jury trial favored Scott's freedom, but the Supreme Court of Missouri reversed the decision and declared Scott a slave. Scott then appealed to the United States Supreme Court. In the Court's 1857 ruling, written by Chief Justice Roger B. Taney, blacks had no right to sue for freedom because they were not and never had been U.S. citizens. Also, in reference to Scott's residence in Illinois, the Court ruled that Congress had no right to ban slavery because slaves were property and as such were protected by the Constitution.

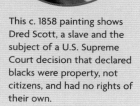

This c. 1858 painting shows Dred Scott, a slave and the subject of a U.S. Supreme Court decision that declared blacks were property, not citizens, and had no rights of their own.

This 1893 painting by Charles T. Webber shows "travelers" who were runaway slaves given refuge at an Underground Railroad safe house "station."

The passage of the Fugitive Slave Act and the Dred Scott decision provoked Douglass to become active in the Underground Railroad. This railroad was not made of steel, but of the iron will and courage of fugitive slaves and the people who led them to freedom. The "railroad" was a series of "stations," or homes, where supportive whites and free blacks, all known as "station masters," hid fugitive slaves, known as "passengers," for a night or more before the fugitives moved on. The Underground Railroad had stations along many escape routes through states in the Northeast and Midwest. Passengers were guided on their journeys by "conductors" who knew the routes. In spite of the best efforts made by passengers and conductors, many slaves were captured or met harm along the way. Yet, it is believed that more than 10,000 runaway slaves traveled the Underground Railroad before the start of the Civil War in 1861.

Harriet Tubman, Railroad Conductor

The most famous and successful conductor of the Underground Railroad was a tiny former slave named Harriet Tubman. In 1848, wealthy Maryland planters offered a reward as high as $40,000 for the capture of this small but very brave black woman. From 1844 through the 1850s, she made more than twenty trips from locations in the South and led more than 300 fugitive slaves to the safety of northern states and Canada. Born into slavery on a farm in Maryland, Harriet was badly mistreated and endured a serious head injury that affected her health for the rest of her life. Harriet rescued not only members of her family but other slaves as well. She was known as the "Moses" of her people by successfully leading them to freedom—just as the biblical Moses had done.

Harriet Tubman was the most famous "conductor" on the Underground Railroad.

Douglass's home was a well-known "station" on the Underground Railroad. It was not unusual for him to arrive at his newspaper office to find one or more frightened people at his doorstep seeking shelter. At times, he and Anna hid as many as eleven "passengers" for at least a night in their home. It is estimated that, over the years, he may have given shelter to hundreds of men and women desperate to escape the bonds of slavery.

A Slave Revolt in Virginia

On October 16, 1859, John Brown, an abolitionist and a leader of the Free-Soil Party, led a band of twenty-one men, both black and white, on a raid of a government armory that stored weapons and other military equipment in the town of Harpers Ferry, Virginia. Brown believed that slaves could only gain their freedom through violent means. Brown and his men took over the armory and captured several residents.

On October 18, U.S. troops, under the command of Colonel Robert E. Lee, stormed the town, killing ten of Brown's men and capturing the other men in his band of raiders. Arrested and tried for **treason**, Brown was found guilty and hanged on December 2, 1859.

The Harpers Ferry raid and a new aggressive campaign against slavery by northern abolitionists had many Southerners worried about the possibility of future slave revolts. Politicians throughout the South held passionate discussions of **secession** from the Union. Some felt that it was time to prepare for war.

In John Brown's doomed 1859 raid at Harpers Ferry, Brown and his men were trapped by gunfire from U.S. troops led by Colonel Robert E. Lee.

Before the raid, Brown had met with Frederick Douglass several times and had begged him to join his raid, but Frederick chose not to participate. Nevertheless, Douglass was accused of being a **conspirator** in planning the revolt. Shortly after John Brown's arrest, federal authorities searched Brown's possessions and found a note from Frederick Douglass, who was giving a lecture in Philadelphia when Brown was arrested. When newspaper headlines covering the Harpers Ferry raid mentioned Douglass's note, Frederick was certain that, as a black man, he would never be given a fair trial to prove his innocence. He quickly returned to his home in Rochester. With the help of friends, he was put on a boat to Canada, barely missing the group of federal marshals who had come looking for him.

From Canada, Douglass sailed to Great Britain in November 1859. Long before having to flee the United States, he had planned to make another lecture tour in Europe. Once in Great Britain, he traveled around England and Scotland and spoke before appreciative audiences. In his speeches, he praised John Brown as a hero who had sacrificed himself to a great cause. Several months later, while preparing for a tour of France, Frederick received news that his youngest child, twelve-year-old Annie, had died. He left for the United States immediately.

Upon his return home, he learned that all criminal charges brought against him for the raid at Harpers Ferry had been dropped. Authorities did not want to cause any more dissension with the abolitionists. Douglass was deeply saddened about losing Annie, the child he referred to as the "light and life of my house," but he was grateful to be back in the United States of America. The country, however, was not to be the *United* States for long.

CHAPTER 10

War! War!

Teach the rebels and traitors that the price they are to pay for the attempt to abolish this government must be the abolition of slavery.

The Republican Party became a national party in 1856, and in the election of 1860, they chose Abraham Lincoln to run as their candidate for president. Of the four candidates who were running at that time, Lincoln was the only one who spoke out against the spread of slavery. But he also supported the relocation of all former slaves to colonies in Africa or Central America. This angered Frederick Douglass, and Lincoln failed to get his support, initially.

In August 1860, Gerrit Smith, a wealthy investor in Douglass's newspaper, entered the presidential election representing the Radical Abolition Party. Unhappy

An 1865 photograph of Abraham Lincoln, who was not Douglass's first choice in the 1860 presidential election.

with Lincoln's stand on relocating free blacks to a colony in Africa, Douglass campaigned for Smith. In the end, however, Douglass voted for Lincoln, because he was convinced that Lincoln had a better chance of beating his Democratic opponent, Stephen A. Douglas. Douglas, a U.S. Senator from Illinois, was supported by voters in the southern states. He maintained that each state should be allowed to make its own decisions about slavery.

Abolitionist Gerrit Smith was a good friend and financial supporter of Frederick Douglass.

Abraham Lincoln won the 1860 election. His victory was one of many reasons why the South threatened to secede, or leave, the Union. Although there were Southerners who did not believe in slavery and were upset about any talk of secession, most Southerners saw Lincoln's victory as a power struggle between the North and the South. For his part, the sixteenth president of the United States refused to believe that the South would leave the Union.

But in December 1860, one month after Lincoln was elected, South Carolina carried out its threat and voted to secede from the United States. Eventually, ten southern states followed suit, and together they formed a new government: the Confederate States of America—also known as the Confederacy. The Confederacy wrote its own constitution and elected as its president Jefferson Davis, a planter and U.S. Senator from Mississippi.

The Civil War Begins

Abraham Lincoln was sworn into office on March 4, 1861. On April 12, Confederate troops being led by General Pierre Beauregard fired on Fort Sumter, which was one of three U.S. government forts in South Carolina that was occupied by Union troops. Cannon blasts between Union and Confederate troops lasted thirty-four hours before Union Major Robert Anderson surrendered the fort and took down the American flag. It was the first battle of the Civil War, and the Confederacy had won it.

At the news of the "firing on the American flag," one newspaper spoke for many Northerners when it declared that "All sympathy with them [the South] is dead!" Few Northerners

This Currier and Ives painting captured the assault and bombing of Fort Sumter in Charleston Harbor on April 12 and 13, 1861.

felt that the South had enough population and industrial power to carry out a war for more than a few months. On the other hand, Southerners saw Northerners as not having the courage or will to maintain a long fight. Both sides were wrong.

Frederick Douglass welcomed the Civil War. He saw the conflict as a fight against states' rights, and as a means to ending the bondage for nearly four million enslaved black people. In a special May 1861 issue of *Douglass' Monthly*, he wrote that the war "called for the arming of both slaves and free blacks." During his lectures, he also called for President Lincoln to emancipate the slaves and wrote: "Teach the rebels and traitors that the price they are to pay for the attempt to abolish this government must be the abolition of slavery."

Lincoln, however, saw the secession of the southern states as an illegal act. The nation was torn apart, and he was determined to restore it. He worried that freeing slaves would encourage the slaveholding Border States—Missouri, Kentucky, West Virginia, Maryland, and Delaware—to join the Confederacy.

Who Could Enlist to Fight?

Filled with a great sense of patriotism, white men in the North enlisted to serve and to defend the Union. At the same time, thousands of able-bodied black men filled their churches and meeting halls in the North to sign up and volunteer. They, too, were eager to join in a fight that they hoped would end slavery.

The Union army told the black volunteers who wanted to enlist that their services would not be needed. Some whites thought that black soldiers would be frightened by cannon fire and would run away from a battle. In truth, racism accounted for the reluctance to enlist black soldiers. General William

Confederate soldiers lay dead along Hagerstown Road after one of the Civil War's deadliest battle at Antietam, Maryland, on September 17, 1862.

Tecumseh Sherman of the Union army demonstrated this racist belief with his comment that a black man could stop a bullet as well as a white man and a sand bag, but, "Can they improvise bridges, sorties [make attacks], flank movements, etc., like the white man. *I* say no."

The Confederate army assigned enslaved blacks in the South to military labor behind the battlefields. On the possibility of having black men serve in the Confederate army, a general from Georgia commented, "You cannot make soldiers of slaves, nor slaves of soldiers. . . . If slaves seem good soldiers, then our whole theory of slavery is wrong."

On September 17, 1862, more than 23,000 Rebel and Yankee soldiers lay dead on the fields of Antietam. It was one of the bloodiest battles in American history, and it had stilled the

Rebels and Yankees

The term *rebel* was originally given to colonists who rebelled against the British government during the American Revolution. So during the Civil War, Confederate soldiers who rebelled against the U.S. government were called "Rebels." Also during the American Revolution, the English used the name *Yankee* as a slang word for American colonists. Colonists and colonial soldiers proudly called themselves "Yankees." A hundred years later, during the Civil War, Southerners called northern soldiers Yankees with scorn. In World War I, which was fought in Europe between 1914 and 1918, English soldiers affectionately called American soldiers "Yanks."

Portrait of Confederate soldier Thomas Kitchen, c. 1861–65, holding a bayonet and rifle.

At the start of many Civil War battles, Yankee and Rebel soldiers would give off battle cries or yells to cheer on their fellow soldiers and to try to frighten off the enemy. These yells could be heard over a long distance, and warned the other side: "Here we come!"

Portrait of Union soldier George Kimbrue, c. 1861–1865, with pistol and saber.

The Confederate yell was known as the "Rebel yell." That was believed to have been a long sound that came off as: "Woh-who-ey! Who-ey! Who-ey! Woh-who-ey!" Union soldiers gave a yell that came off as "*Hoo*-ray! *Hoo*-ray! *Hoo*-ray!" None of these yells were sounds the other side wanted to hear.

This illustration shows President Abraham Lincoln reading a draft of the Emancipation Proclamation to his cabinet during the summer of 1862.

battle cries of the people on both sides of the conflict. Though the combat had been a major Union victory, the public in the North was beginning to lose support for the Civil War.

Tears of Joy

Less than a week after the Battle of Antietam, Lincoln called his cabinet into his office to reveal a powerful document that he had written. If the war did not end by the new year of 1863, this document would end slavery. The war and its bloodshed continued through the fall and winter, and Lincoln's document, the Emancipation Proclamation, became law on January 1, 1863. It stated that people held as slaves in Confederate states and those who fled the South would be "forever free."

To the disappointment of Frederick Douglass and many other abolitionists, the Emancipation was written to end slavery in the Confederacy. It did not apply to slaveholding Border States that had stayed in the Union. Lincoln had wanted to reward those states for staying loyal. He also feared that had he forced slaveholders in the Border States to free their slaves, the states would have gone over to the Confederacy.

The signing of the Emancipation Proclamation made New Year's 1863 a great day for anyone who supported the end of slavery. Frederick Douglass was in Boston, one of several cities where huge celebrations were planned. Three thousand people had gathered at each of two large auditoriums: the Boston Music Hall and the Tremont Temple. There were whites and blacks, many of them abolitionists, at both locations. Everyone was determined to stay until they heard official word that the Emancipation Proclamation had been signed.

Just before midnight, a Boston judge, Thomas Russell, rushed to a telegraph office, then ran back to Tremont Temple, carrying Lincoln's announcement. It read in part: "I do order and declare that all persons held as slaves . . . henceforward shall be free."

"I do order and declare that all persons held as slaves . . . henceforward shall be free."

Frederick Douglass and William Lloyd Garrison, standing on the stage, wept. Harriet Beecher Stowe, whose novel *Uncle Tom's Cabin* had gained worldwide support for the abolitionist cause in America, rose from her seat. She stood with tears in her eyes after the crowd called her name to stand. In describing his emotion at the time, Frederick Douglass said, "I never saw joy before. Men, women, young and old, were up; hats and bonnets were in the air."

Freedom had come for some. Douglass saw that there remained one more struggle: To take on the fight to free all slaves, and he encouraged blacks to join in the fight. That meant putting on a Union uniform. When asked during his lecture circuits why blacks should enlist, he replied, "You will stand more erect, feel more at ease, and be less liable to insult than you ever were before."

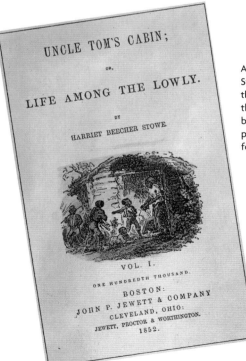

A cover of Harriet Beecher Stowe's *Uncle Tom's Cabin*—the 1852 novel that depicted the evils of slavery. It became a best-seller and caused many people to demand social justice for African Americans.

CHAPTER 11

Fighting for Military Equality

Once the black man get[s] . . . a musket on his shoulder and bullets in his pockets . . . no power on earth . . . can deny that he has earned the right of citizenship in the United States.

After the Emancipation Proclamation, the Union army actively recruited black soldiers. Douglass was overjoyed with this new turn of events. He believed that

"Once the black man get[s] . . . a musket on his shoulder and bullets in his pockets . . . no power on earth . . . can deny that he has earned the right of citizenship in the United States." More than 186,000 black soldiers were soon organized into 166 troop units called regiments. Many black Union soldiers were runaway slaves who came

Two African American soldiers were photographed, c. 1860–1870, wearing their Union army uniforms.

from Border States. The most famous of these black Civil War units was the Fifty-Fourth Massachusetts Regiment. Douglass himself recruited many of its men and included two of his sons—Charles and Lewis.

Robert Gould Shaw, a white man and the son of wealthy Boston abolitionists, was appointed captain of the Fifty-Fourth Massachusetts. On May 28, 1863, thousands of people lined Boston's streets and rooftops to cheer their support for the regiment as it marched to war. On that day, perhaps no father was prouder of his sons than Frederick Douglass.

After displaying their bravery in several battles, black troops began earning the respect of white troops. But they did not earn the same pay. The lowest ranking white soldier was paid

Two black Union soldiers are shown firing their rifles in Dutch Gap, Virginia, 1864.

thirteen dollars a month while all black soldiers, no matter their rank or experience, were paid ten dollars. Douglass learned that they were not only underpaid, but that they were also not given the same food and clothing allowances. Blacks were not given—as whites had been—a bounty, or signing-up reward, for enlisting.

Out of 186,000 black soldiers, fewer than one hundred were officers. Although black troops suffered from inequality, there were still a number of Civil War heroes among them. One such hero was Robert Smalls, a former slave who was forced to work on a Confederate ship but eventually became ship captain in the Union fleet.

The South was angry about the Union's use of black troops. To make examples of them and their white officers, the Confederate congress passed a new ordinance, or law, in 1863, stating that captured armed black Union soldiers would be killed or enslaved. None were to be considered "prisoners of war," which would allow them to be held in a prison camp until the end of the war. White officers of black regiments were to be shot on the spot. Douglass was shocked that there was no response of outrage from the White House about this type of brutality against black soldiers. He asked, "What has Mr. Lincoln to say about this slavery and murder? What has he said? Not one word."

The number of black men enlisting began to drop. Angered by Lincoln's silence, Douglass didn't feel that he could encourage men to join an army that would not support all of its men. Finally, Lincoln responded to the ordinance by accusing the Confederates of being **barbarians**. He said that civilized nations did not treat prisoners of war differently based on their color. Lincoln then threatened: "For every United States soldier killed in violation of the laws of war, a rebel soldier would be executed."

A Black Navy Hero

At the beginning of the Civil War, Robert Smalls, a former slave from a South Carolina plantation was forced to serve as a wheelman on the *Planter*, an armed Confederate ship. He was responsible for steering the ship, and on the night of May 12, 1862, he and twelve slaves serving aboard the *Planter* seized control of the vessel. Smalls guided the ship out of Charleston Harbor, passing Confederate guns and cannons that guarded it. He then delivered the *Planter* to the fleet of Union ships that were blocking the entrance to the city of Charleston.

The Union army took over the *Planter* and hired Smalls to work as the pilot of the ship. During a surprise attack by Confederates, the white Union captain of the ship tried to surrender the *Planter*, but Smalls locked him in a coal storage room and once again guided the ship past heavy cannon fire. For Small's bravery, the Union army named him the captain of the *Planter*.

Robert Smalls, born a slave in Beaufort, South Carolina, became a Civil War hero for the Union side. He later served five terms in the U.S. Congress.

Following the Civil War, Smalls served in the South Carolina House of Representatives and in the state's senate. In 1875, he was elected to the U.S. Congress.

A Visit to Washington, D.C.

In July 1863, Frederick Douglass visited Washington, D.C., for the first time. He went there to meet with members of Congress to discuss the concerns of black soldiers. Senator Samuel C. Pomeroy of Kansas took Douglass to meet Secretary of War Edwin M. Stanton. At their meeting, Douglass requested that blacks receive equal pay and promotions. Although Stanton gave his word that he would do what he could, a law giving equal pay to black soldiers was not passed until June 1864.

At a later meeting, Stanton asked Frederick Douglass to join the army as an assistant adjutant general under General Lorenzo Thomas. He would be responsible for recruiting black soldiers in the Mississippi Valley and would receive the respectable sum of one hundred dollars a month, plus money for his transportation and his expenses. But the War Department denied Douglass the rank of officer; he would have to serve as a civilian. Douglass turned the offer down. He said that he knew the "value of [an officer's] shoulder straps " and would not go into the army without "some visible mark of my rank."

Edwin M. Stanton was secretary of war in President Abraham Lincoln's cabinet.

On August 10, 1863, Frederick Douglass met with President Abraham Lincoln. Only moments after presenting his card at the White House, Douglass was led directly into Lincoln's office.

He was not made to wait in a long line, as was the practice when someone wanted an audience with the president. Apparently Douglass's reputation as the nation's leading black abolitionist enabled him to bypass the large crowd in the hall.

Upon entering the room, Douglass noticed that Lincoln was surrounded by books, papers, and several secretaries who were busy working for the president. Lincoln was seated in a low armchair. As the president began to rise, Douglass started to introduce himself. "I know who you are, Mr. Douglass," Lincoln said. "Mr. Seward [William H.; Secretary of State] has told me all about you. Sit down. I am glad to see you."

On August 10, 1863, Frederick Douglass met with President Abraham Lincoln.

Douglass immediately launched into his appeal for equal pay and promotions for black soldiers. He also wanted revenge to be taken against captured Confederate soldiers who would enslave or kill black prisoners of war. Having listened in silence, but with great sympathy, Lincoln admitted that he, too, was troubled by Frederick's concerns. He told Douglass that black soldiers had certainly proven themselves on the battlefields, and that he would see to it that they received pay raises and **commissions**.

But Lincoln could not promise to carry out his threats of revenge against rebel soldiers. He could not bear the thought of hanging a Confederate soldier for a crime committed by his fellow soldiers. "Once started, where would such **retaliation** end?" Though not completely satisfied with this answer, Douglass believed that Lincoln had "the tender heart of a man rather than the stern warrior and commander-in-chief of the American Army and Navy."

The March to Fort Wagner

At the time that Frederick Douglass was in Washington **lobbying** for equal pay and rank for black soldiers, the Fifty-Fourth Massachusetts regiment was making its way to Fort Wagner in South Carolina. They would be the lead unit in an attack on this Confederate fortress. Douglass's sons were in the regiment, and it was expected that the regiment would suffer high **casualties** with this assault.

Although the regiment lost 270 men, Douglass's sons survived the storming of Fort Wagner. Describing the fight, Lewis Douglass wrote: "Men fell all around me. A shell would explode and clear a space of twenty feet, our men would close up again, but it was no use; we had to retreat, which was a very hazardous undertaking. How I got out of the fight alive, I cannot tell, but I am here."

Slavery Is Abolished

Although the Emancipation Proclamation had freed all slaves in Confederate states, President Lincoln was not confident that these southern states would live up to this declaration, especially if they were victorious. He would have to develop a plan to rescue former slaves living in the South.

Lincoln invited Frederick Douglass to the White House to talk about playing a part in the rescue. Shortly after that meeting Douglass sent Lincoln a letter describing his strategy, but with the Union's battle success in Georgia and South Carolina, Lincoln never had to use the plan. In 1864, President Abraham Lincoln was reelected for a second term, and on January 31, 1865, Congress voted to pass the Thirteenth Amendment—an addition to the Constitution—that would abolish slavery.

Assault on Fort Wagner

As the 650 members of Fifty-Fourth Massachusetts approached Fort Wagner, eight units of white Union soldiers followed the black regiment. The assault was especially dangerous for the men of the Fifty-Fourth. They had seen very little battle, and they had never taken on an enemy fort.

The battle began on July 18, 1863, when soldiers of the Fifty-Fourth ran across a strip of sandy beach toward Fort Wagner. They were met with heavy Confederate fire, and many men were killed on the beach. When the soldiers of the black regiment reached the fort, Robert Shaw, the young captain of the Fifty-Fourth was killed.

A flag bearer of a white Union regiment was also killed, but as he fell, Sergeant William Carney, a former slave, snatched up the American flag and crawled to safety while bullets hit him in his head, chest, and right arm. Carney survived and was the first of twenty-three black Civil War soldiers to receive the Congressional Medal of Honor.

This print, c. 1890, shows the black Union soldiers of the Massachusetts Fifty-Fourth storming Fort Wagner. The regiment lost 270 men that day.

A light rain fell on the morning of March 4, 1865, the day that Lincoln was sworn into office for a second time. As the man the public fondly nicknamed "Honest Abe" stepped forward, the rain clouds faded and the sun appeared. Standing proudly in the inaugural crowd was Frederick Douglass. The Civil War was coming to an end, and the Union was expected to win. Douglass had faith that Lincoln's leadership would be valuable in helping black people—both in the North and the South—gain equality as American citizens. Lincoln spoke of wanting to rebuild the South and "bind up the wounds . . . and achieve a lasting peace." Douglass believed that newly freed blacks could benefit from this peace and have a part in that rebuilding

More than 50,000 people gathered to watch President Abraham Lincoln take the oath of office at his second inauguration, as shown in this wood engraving.

CHAPTER 12

Freedom Without Equality

Slavery is not abolished until the black man has the ballot [to vote].

A grand reception was held at the White House on the evening of Lincoln's inauguration. It was an opportunity that allowed the public to meet and congratulate the president and his wife, Mary Todd Lincoln. Frederick Douglass was one of thousands who pressed forward to enter the mansion. Many other black people had also hoped to attend the reception, but it had been a longstanding rule that people of color were not allowed

Abraham and Mary Todd Lincoln are shown enjoying their inauguration reception in this 1865 colored lithograph.

to participate in the White House reception, so the police did not admit them.

As Douglass approached the entrance, two policemen grabbed him. He told them that if Mr. Lincoln knew he was there, the president would order them to admit him. Breaking from their grip, Douglass ran into the hallway but was seized by two other policemen. He asked them to "Just say to Mr. Lincoln that Fred Douglass is at the door."

Douglass was quickly taken into the elegant East Room of the White House, which was filled with men and women in formal clothes.Holding out his to hand to shake Frederick's, Lincoln, stood tall, appearing—Douglass thought—"as a mountain pine, high above everyone else in the room." As Douglass approached the president, Lincoln said, "Here comes my friend Douglass. I am glad to see you. I saw you in the crowd today listening to my inaugural address." He asked Frederick what he thought of his speech. Frederick reminded the president that there were thousands of people waiting to shake his hand.

Lincoln said, "You must stop a little Douglass; there is no man in the country whose opinion I value more than yours. I want to know what you thought of it?" After Frederick said that he liked the speech, both men shook hands and Douglass left. It was the last time he saw Lincoln alive.

The End of the War and Lincoln

In April 1865, Union forces of 125,000 men led by General Ulysses S. Grant surrounded 35,000 Confederate soldiers led by General Robert E. Lee. On April 2, Grant and his army captured the Confederate capital of Richmond, Virginia. On the ninth of that month, General Lee surrendered to Grant at the Appomattox Court House in Virginia. More than three million soldiers—Union and

This 1865 lithograph by Currier and Ives shows Abraham Lincoln being assassinated by John Wilkes Booth at Ford's Theatre in Washington, D.C.

Confederate—had fought in the Civil War, and 620,000 had died. Of those numbers, about 38,000 black men had lost their lives.

On the evening of Friday, April 14, 1865, President and Mrs. Lincoln attended a play at Washington's Ford's Theatre. During the performance, a man named John Wilkes Booth shot President Lincoln in the head, then jumped onto the stage and ran away. The assassin blamed Lincoln for destroying the Confederacy and for bringing an end to slavery. Abraham Lincoln never recovered from his injuries. He died the next morning, on April 15, at 7:22 a.m.

Frederick Douglass was crushed by Lincoln's assassination. Months later, a grieving Mary Todd Lincoln presented certain possessions that had belonged to her husband to special people. She gave Frederick Douglass Lincoln's favorite walking stick. She was thought to have said: "I know no one that would appreciate this more than Fred Douglass."

As the nation prepared to bury Abraham Lincoln in April 1865, Vice President Andrew Johnson, a former U.S. Senator from Tennessee, was sworn in as president. Although Johnson was a Democrat from Tennessee, Lincoln, a Republican, had chosen Johnson to be his vice president. Johnson was a powerful politician and the only southern senator to remain loyal to the Union.

Black Code Laws

Although African Americans in the South were now free, they were not given the same rights as whites. In fact, they were treated harshly by local governments. To control their now-free black population, southern legislatures passed Black Code laws. These laws restricted the political, economic, and social lives of black people. Black Code laws forbade African Americans to purchase land, and they were not permitted to hold certain jobs. At the same time, an unemployed black adult could be fined or arrested and jailed. Blacks were also not allowed to hold meetings unless a white person was in attendance. Worse, they were denied the right to vote. The Black Code laws placed African Americans back into another kind of enslavement. Despite Johnson's promise to follow Lincoln's plans for rebuilding the South, he was unwilling to improve the conditions of blacks in the South.

To control their now-free black population, southern legislatures passed Black Code laws.

In the meantime, blacks were also losing direct support from their defenders in the North. Only a month after the Civil War ended, William Lloyd Garrison, among other abolitionists, called to discontinue the American Anti-Slavery Society. He believed

After the Civil War, the South enacted Black Code laws that fined unemployed blacks. This 1867 engraving shows a freed man trying to sell his services in order to pay his fine.

that it had achieved its goal of helping to end slavery. Frederick Douglass angrily responded by writing that, "Slavery is not abolished until the black man has the ballot [to vote]."

The Freedmen's Bureau

In 1865, Congress created the Freedmen's Bureau. The bureau assisted millions of newly free blacks and poor whites living in war-torn cities and on farms in the South. Its purpose was to provide, for one year, food, clothing, shelter, medical care, and jobs to needy people. The bureau also created more than one thousand public schools throughout the South and several colleges for black students.

An 1866 engraving shows a classroom at the Freedmen's Bureau school in Vicksburg, Mississippi. Students of all ages attended and were eager to learn.

Frederick Douglass's son Charles was hired to work as a clerk at the bureau's headquarters in Washington and was paid a salary of one hundred dollars a month. General Oliver O. Howard, the bureau's white director, later admitted to Charles that the bureau's white clerks had protested when they learned a black man would be hired. In response, Howard had threatened to fire them and "fill their places with colored men."

A year later, Congress voted to extend money to keep the Freedmen's Bureau operating. President Johnson **vetoed** the extension, but Congress overrode his veto. The bureau operated for six more years. At one point, black residents in Washington demanded that the bureau hire a black man to run the organization. When Douglass was offered the job, he turned it down. This was a federal government job, and he felt that he couldn't work for President Johnson, a man he didn't trust.

More Constitutional Amendments

In February 1866, Douglass, his son Lewis, and a group of black leaders met with Andrew Johnson in Washington to protest the Black Codes that were making life miserable for blacks in the South. Speaking for the group, Douglass mentioned how Abraham Lincoln had been a "noble and humane" leader. He continued saying that as black people had been called to serve in the war to save the Union, they should be given the vote to "save ourselves." Johnson was offended by the black leader's remarks and ignored his plea. It was Johnson's opinion that he had already gone to greater lengths than he felt that he should have for black people.

Douglass was not discouraged by the cold reception from the president. He continued to focus a new round of lectures on the issue of **civil rights** for blacks.

He continued to focus a new round of lectures on the issue of civil rights for blacks.

In 1868, when Congress passed the Fourteenth Amendment, President Johnson vetoed it. This law would grant citizenship to all people born in the United States, regardless of color. Congress overrode Johnson's veto. Two years later, Congress also passed the Fifteenth Amendment, which provided that no man could be denied the right to vote based on his color.

Distrustful of Johnson's failed attempts to rebuild the South, Congress took charge of the South's **Reconstruction**. In 1867, it passed the First Reconstruction Act, which divided the South into five military districts controlled by the Union army.

A commander in each district had the power to guarantee the voting rights for black men. To rejoin the Union, each of the former Confederate states had to write a new constitution that guaranteed voting rights to all men. And their governments had to approve the Fourteenth Amendment.

During the eleven years of Reconstruction, some African Americans in southern states did enjoy certain freedoms, such as voting and participating in the political process. In 1867 and 1868, southern states drew up their most **progressive** constitutions. Most removed the requirement that voters had to be property owners. All males, regardless of color, were entitled to vote.

Under the Fifteenth Amendment, black men were guaranteed the right to vote for the first time, as shown in this 1867 engraving.

Black Politicians

More than 600 African Americans were elected to public office during Reconstruction. Most served in their state legislature. Black politicians had the greatest numbers of voters and political power in South Carolina, where two black men were also elected to serve as black lieutenant governors, in 1870 and 1872. Forty black men in Mississippi were elected to the state legislature.

The state also elected the first two black senators to the U.S. Congress: Hiram R. Revels, a clergyman and teacher, and Blanche K. Bruce, who earlier had established a school for black children in Missouri. There were

During Reconstruction, African Americans elected to Congress included Hiram R. Revels, a clergyman and educator from Mississippi who became the first African American U.S. senator.

also black congressional representatives from Alabama, Florida, Georgia, Louisiana, Mississippi, North Carolina, and South Carolina.

African American legislators in Congress and in southern state capitals worked to help black citizens on issues concerning education, **suffrage**, and employment. Not just concerned with issues affecting black people, they also introduced bills that would help Native Americans and programs that would help improve their home-state communities.

Many African Americans ran for office and won their elections. Still, African Americans lived through trying times during Reconstruction. Some moved north, but most remained where they had lived before the war. To survive, they, like poor whites, became sharecroppers. Former plantation owners who had lost their wealth but were land rich divided their property into plots of land that they rented to poor farmers who had to share their crops with the landowners. Some sharecroppers had to give up as much as half of the crops they grew to pay the rent.

Klan Violence

Even after the war, southern whites feared that there would be an uprising of free blacks. However, no such event happened. Instead, during Reconstruction, some black politicians, such as Senator Hiram R. Revels, of Mississippi, took action to abolish laws that had deprived former Confederates leaders of the right to vote or to hold office. And instead of violence *from* black communities, there was

Black Code laws in the South gave rise to the Ku Klux Klan, a group that was determined to "keep the black man in his place" through terror and violence.

increased violence *against* African Americans. The Ku Klux Klan, a secret society of long southern men, did their best to terrorize blacks. Dressed in long robes and head coverings, they burned homes and **lynched** blacks they felt "got out of line." To keep black children from receiving an education, the Klan burned their schools and murdered their teachers. But the desire to learn among the former slaves was so strong that it was possible to see both young and old—even grandparents—learning alongside their grandchildren in the same classroom.

During Andrew Johnson's last two years in office, Congress and the American public had both turned against him. It seemed as if Johnson wanted to block any legislation that would help the new black citizens. Congress finally tried to **impeach** him. But in his impeachment hearing, Congress failed by one vote, and Johnson served out his remaining two years with little power.

A New President

In 1868, Frederick Douglass campaigned for Ulysses S. Grant, the former Commander in Chief of the Union army during the Civil War. Grant ran as the Republican candidate for president. Frederick had grown increasingly uneasy about the Democratic Party's lack of interest in the difficulties of blacks in the South. His advice to blacks was to "stick to the Republican Party . . . [and] do your utmost to keep it in power in state and nation."

Douglass's active campaign for Grant helped bring in a large black vote for the Republican Party, and Ulysses S. Grant won the presidency. Douglass was thanked for his contributions to the party, and he thought that he would be rewarded with a political appointment. He had hoped for a position that would give him the power to hire blacks for government jobs. None was offered.

Douglass supported Ulysses S. Grant in the 1868 presidential election. This 1869 campaign poster shows Grant and Schuyler Colfax who ran as the vice-presidential candidate.

After beginning another lecture tour in 1871, fifty-three-year-old Frederick Douglass proudly accepted an invitation by Grant to join a delegation with four white men to visit Santo Domingo, which is now named the Dominican Republic. President Grant was interested in having the island join the United States as a territory. When the group returned, Grant invited the four white men of the group to dinner at the White House, but he left out Douglass. Frederick covered his deep disappointment and instead praised the president as a great supporter of black civil rights.

A Series of Misfortunes

In the meantime, Douglass was plagued with a series of misfortunes. In 1870, he served as the editor of the *New National Era*, a newspaper with a black readership that was published in Washington, D.C. The paper went out of business four years later, but not before Douglass published his opinions about race relations and reported on the progress that blacks had made around the country.

In 1872, his house in Rochester was set afire by arsonists. No one had been injured, but having lived in the community for more than twenty-five years, Douglass was stunned that someone wanted to burn down his home. The fire destroyed irreplaceable copies of his *North Star* newspapers. Since he spent much of his time working in Washington, D.C., he and Anna bought a home there.

In 1872, his house in Rochester was set afire by arsonists.

After moving to Washington, Douglass served on the board of trustees of the Freedman's Savings and Trust Company. The bank was created by Congress to help blacks gain financial responsibility. After joining, he accepted an offer to become the bank's president. Frederick was pleased to be in a position that could help black people develop financial security. But with no experience in banking, and having only served on the board for a short time, he was unaware that the bank was on the threshold of **bankruptcy**.

In the summer of 1874, the bank closed. Hundreds of black people lost their savings, and they blamed Douglass. He was humiliated and greatly saddened for the hard-working investors who lost their money. He, too, had also lost money, but he was richer than some of the other investors.

In 1877, Douglass returned to St. Michaels, Maryland, to see members of his family and friends and to come face-to-face with his painful past. Hearing of Douglass's visit to St. Michaels, Thomas Auld, the man who once owned him, invited Frederick to his home. Auld, who was quite old and sick, wept at the sight of his former slave. Frederick also became so moved emotionally that he could not speak for several minutes. When the two men were able to talk, the years seemed to pass away. Auld was weak, but his thinking was clear.

At one point, Auld said he always knew that Frederick was too smart to be a slave. He told him ". . . had I been in your place, I should have done as you did." Auld told Frederick that he had followed news of his life and career. Frederick asked the old man about the date of his birth. Thomas told him that Frederick was born in February 1818. At the end of their twenty-minute meeting, the bitterness that both men had carried for years had faded.

An 1885 oil-painted photograph shows a dignified Frederick Douglass with his mane of white hair.

CHAPTER 13

Fighting for Justice to the End

Men talk of the Negro problem. There is no Negro problem. The problem is whether the American people have loyalty enough, honor enough, patriotism enough to live up to their own Constitution.

Sixty-year-old Frederick Douglass and his wife, Anna, moved again in 1878. This time their home was a fourteen-room house in Washington surrounded by nine acres of land. The large house with tall white columns sat near the banks of the Anacostia section of the Potomac River. Douglass filled his home with portraits of the famous people he had known and admired, including Abraham Lincoln and William Lloyd Garrison. He spent many pleasurable hours reading and working in his book-filled library. The Douglasses named the house Cedar Hill, and they enjoyed their children's frequent visits.

After President Grant left office, Douglass continued to campaign hard for the Republican presidential candidates. As the nation's most famous black man, Douglass served as an unpaid adviser to Presidents Rutherford B. Hayes and James A. Garfield on issues concerning African Americans.

Frederick Douglass spent many hours at his desk in his book-lined library at Cedar Hill.

President Hayes made Douglass a U.S. marshal, or federal officer, for the District of Columbia. He also became the city's recorder of legal papers—called deeds—during Garfield's short term. (James Garfield was assassinated nine months after taking office.) Neither position offered to Douglass was considered an important appointment.

Douglass wrote his third autobiography, *Life and Times of Frederick Douglass*, in 1881. In the book, he covered the history of the nation during the Civil War and the plight of freed blacks. Unlike his earlier books, *Life and Times* was not a best-seller during his lifetime.

Douglass Remarries

In July 1882, Anna Murray Douglass suffered a stroke and died a month later. During their forty-three-year marriage, Anna had led a very private life while her husband led a very public life. On her passing, Douglass commented that Anna was the center of their home and the person who had held the family together.

Anna's death left Frederick shaken and depressed. In time, he returned to his busy life; and a year later he fell in love with Helen Pitts, a white woman who was twenty years younger than Frederick. They

Helen Pitts was Frederick Douglass's second wife and was active in the women's rights movement.

had often met while attending suffragette meetings. Once again, gossip abounded when Helen went to work in his office and even more so when they married on January 24, 1884.

Both whites and blacks were critical of the marriage, and white politicians even called for a ban on mixed marriages in the District of Columbia. Helen's father and Frederick's children, especially his oldest daughter, Rosetta, could not forgive the couple for marrying. Douglass chose to ignore the chatter and outrage. He felt that Helen was his equal in her dedication to working for the same causes. For her part, Helen said, "Love came to me and I was not afraid to marry the man I loved because of his color."

During much of 1886, the couple traveled abroad in Great Britain, where they visited his old friends. They toured France, Italy, Greece, and Egypt, and then returned to Washington and Cedar Hill.

A Giant Step Backward

Returning to the United States, Douglass visited South Carolina and Georgia and saw firsthand the desperate conditions in which black sharecroppers and their families lived. It was obvious that the Fourteenth and Fifteenth Amendments had not brought an era of freedom to that region. In fact, five years after Congress passed the Civil Rights Act of 1875, which called for equal treatment in public places, the U.S. Supreme Court struck it down, ruling that discrimination practiced by individuals was legal.

It was obvious that the Fourteenth and Fifteenth Amendments had not brought an era of freedom to that region.

Douglass returned to a lecture tour and, employing the fiery oration of his youth, described how these needy people were being denied their civil rights. He also regained respect from those who had thought that Douglass had strayed from his lifelong cause.

Reconstruction had ended in 1877. Southern conservatives had regained political power in Congress and in their state governments, and Northerners were beginning to lose interest in the causes of former slaves. With low public support for the Reconstruction program, newly elected Rutherford B. Hayes put an end to it by withdrawing federal troops from the South. Now free from the unwelcome control and power of the hated North, local governments in the South refused to accept the law as described in the Fourteenth and Fifteenth Amendments. In their place came the Jim Crow laws, which legalized segregation and separated blacks and whites at schools and jobs, in housing, and in all other areas of daily life. Most of the gains that blacks had made during Reconstruction were done away with.

A Diplomat in Haiti

Benjamin Harrison assumed the presidency in 1889. That year, Harrison appointed Douglass as a diplomat to represent the interests of the United States on the Caribbean island of Haiti. Douglass's full title was "minister resident and consul general to Haiti." The island was once a French possession, but it had won its independence during a revolt of its large slave population in 1804.

Douglass was honored to represent the United States in a country that was the world's oldest black republic. Like in the United States, the people of Haiti elected their government officials. Douglass was also pleased to serve in a country where ancestors of nearly all of the population had been African slaves who were brought to the island. The Haitians were pleased to have the famous champion of American rights in their midst.

Douglass and the Haitian President Florvil Hyppolite were on good terms. However, when President Harrison asked Douglass

A photograph of Florvil Hyppolite, President of the Republic of Haiti at the time Frederick Douglass served as Minister Resident and Counsul General to Haiti.

to set up an agreement with Haiti to use its largest port as a refueling station for the U.S. Navy, the Haitian government refused. They feared the naval base would allow the United States to dominate their small island-nation. American newspapers blamed Douglass's failure to secure the agreement on his lack of skills in **diplomacy**. The public maintained this opinion even though a U.S. Navy admiral was later sent on the same mission and also failed.

A Last Fight

Douglass, who was now seventy-three years old, resigned from the position in 1891 and returned home. Once back at Cedar Hill, he and Helen lived a quiet life. They spent evenings with invited guests who listened to family concerts performed by Frederick playing the violin and Helen playing the piano.

Frederick still gave occasional lectures and spoke out against issues that negatively affected the rights and lives of blacks and women at risk. At the Chicago **World's Fair** in 1893, he discovered that there was no exhibit featuring the contributions of African Americans. Douglass requested a Colored People's Day at the

A lithograph, c. 1893, shows the opening of the Chicago World's Fair in 1893. President Grover Cleveland is shown in the bottom inset.

exhibition to honor black artists. Instead of displaying the works of poets and painters, the organizers put up watermelon stands. These stands represented a racist stereotype that was fostered by insulting nineteenth-century postcards and political cartoons of black children with huge, hideous grins standing in a patch of watermelons.

Douglass was scheduled to speak that day at the exhibition on "The Race Problem in America." As he stood before the audience, white men at the rear of the hall shouted to drown out his voice. He was stopped for a minute by their rudeness. Then Douglass stood tall, his full mane of white hair surrounding his proud face, and in his deep voice, Frederick began a moving speech that lasted an hour.

"Men talk of the Negro problem," he said. "There is no Negro problem. The problem is whether the American people have loyalty enough, honor enough, patriotism enough to live up to their own Constitution." Ending his oration, the audience gave him a standing applause.

During the 1890s, Douglass continued to write and lecture for causes that stirred his interest. One such concern was the growing incidents of violence against African Americans in the South. He supported Ida B. Wells, a young black publisher who used her newspapers to crusade against such brutality.

A Man Among Men

A loyal supporter of women's rights, Douglass addressed a Washington meeting of the National Council of Women on February 20, 1895. That evening he returned to Cedar Hill and, during dinner, suddenly crumpled to the floor. A few moments later, Frederick Douglass lay dead of a heart attack. He was seventy-seven years old.

Ida B. Wells (1862-1931)

Ida B. Wells was a newspaper editor, journalist, and suffragist during the late nineteenth century. She was born in 1862, a daughter of slaves in Mississippi. Ida was educated at schools—including Fisk University—that were created for black students during the Reconstruction era. While traveling on a train in 1884, twenty-two-year-old Ida was pulled from her seat in a "white ladies only" car and given the choice to move to the Jim Crow car for blacks or a smoking car. Ida put up a fight and was taken off the train. This incident started her crusade to fight the injustices directed at African Americans. When Ida wrote about her experience, black newspapers around the country carried her story. She became a journalist believing that educating people on how to fight against injustice would bring change.

Writing for newspapers in Chicago and New York, Ida wrote editorials about the lynching of black men by white mobs around the country. She encouraged black people to protest lynching by boycotting white businesses. Ignoring death threats, the fearless woman publicly spoke out in the United States and in Europe against these assaults and insisted that local governments step in to help stop them. Ida B. Wells was also a founder of the National Association for the Advancement of Colored People (NAACP) in 1909—an organization that continues to fight for equal rights today.

Ida B. Wells became a well-known black journalist who fought against injustice and brought the problems of black people to the public's attention.

Schools attended by black children in Washington, D.C., were closed for four days after Douglass's death. Thousands of people, rich and poor, ordinary citizens and famous ones from around the country filed past his casket at the Metropolitan African Methodist Episcopal Church. All had come to see, for the last time, one of the most famous men of the nineteenth century.

After his funeral, Helen and the Douglass children accompanied his body to Rochester, where he lay on view in City Hall. Frederick Douglass was buried at Rochester's Mount Hope Cemetery, near his first wife, Anna, and their daughter Annie.

Frederick Douglass was America's first great civil rights leader. He threw off the physical, mental, and legal chains of slavery and became one of America's greatest champions for human rights. It was said that his life was proof that once black people could read and write about their injustices, they would have the power to end slavery.

A very public man, Douglass sometimes cherished just being Fred Douglass. During his visit to Italy—where he was probably not well known—he reflected in an expanded edition of *Life and Times of Frederick Douglass*. He wrote "after my life of hardships in slavery and of conflict with race and color prejudice and [criticism] at home, there was left to me a space in life when I could and did walk the world unquestioned, a man among men."

The grave site of Frederick Douglass is located at Mount Hope Cemetery, in Rochester, New York.

Glossary

abolition—the end of slavery.

apprentice—a beginner who works with an expert to learn a trade.

bankruptcy—the state of having no money.

barbarians—crude or brutal people.

casualties—people who have been injured or killed.

civil rights—the rights that allow people to be treated equally.

commissions—assignments to officer ranks.

compromise—to settle a disagreement by having each side give up something.

conspirator—a person who makes secret plans.

copybooks—books showing handwriting for students to copy.

Deep South—cotton-growing states in the nineteenth century, including South Carolina, Georgia, Alabama, and Mississippi.

diplomacy—the practice of developing good relationships with other countries.

humiliating—to be extremely embarrassing.

impeach—to remove a public official for wrongdoings.

investment—the act of putting one's money or other resources to good use.

lobbying—influencing legislators for certain causes.

lynched—to be seized by a mob and killed, usually by hanging.

manumission—the act of freeing a person.

orators—people who are excellent speakers.

prejudiced—having an unfavorable opinion about someone based solely on race.

progressive—very forward thinking or lenient.

Quaker—a member of the Society of Friends, a Christian religion founded in the seventeenth century.

Reconstruction—the period after the Civil War when Congress passed laws to rebuild the South and bring southern states back into Union.

retaliation—responding in a tough or unkind way.

scandal—a shocking event or behavior.

secession—the act of withdrawing from a group or organization.

suffrage—the right to vote.

treason—the act of betraying one's government.

vetoed—when a governor or president has rejected a bill passed by a legislative body.

World's Fair—a large fair that features the cultural exhibits of many countries.

Bibliography

Books

Burchard, Peter. *Lincoln and Slavery*. New York: Atheneum Books for Children, 1999.

Douglass, Frederick. *Narrative of the Life of Frederick Douglass, an American Slave, Written by Himself*. New York: Norton, 1997.

Fleming, Alice. *Frederick Douglass: From Slave to Statesman*. New York: Rosen PowerKids Press, 2004.

Lester, Julius. *To Be a Slave*. New York: Scholastic Inc., 1968.

Russell, Sharman Apt. *Frederick Douglas: Abolitionist*. New York: Chelsea House Publishers, 1988.

U.S. Department of the Interior, Official Park Service Handbook. *Underground Railroad*.

Ward, Geoffrey C., with Rick and Ken Burns. *The Civil War: An Illustrated History*. New York: Alfred A. Knopf, 2000.

Videotapes

Fredrick Douglass: When the Lion Wrote History, PBS Home Video, VHS, directed by Orlando Bagwell. Washington, D.C.: WTAE, Suiteland, MD: ROJA Productions, 1994.

Frederick Douglass, A&E Biography VHS, Hollywood, CA: Greystone Communications, 1997.

Image Credits

About the Author

Frances E. Ruffin is the author of more than thirty nonfiction books for
children, including a Children's Choices Selection for 2006. She was
especially pleased to write about Frederick Douglass, who was one of her
father's heroes. Ms. Ruffin lives in New York City.

Index

Abolition, 36, 120
Abolitionist movement. *See also specific abolitionist names*
  blows to, 72–76
  center of, 40
  Emancipation Proclamation and, 85–87, 94
  European abolitionists and, 56
  Fifth of July speech, 70–71
  hatred of, 52–53
  Julia Griffiths scandal and, 67
  Massachusetts Anti-Slavery Society and, 49–52
  Quakers and, 46, 50, 120
Abolition of slavery, 94
American Colonization Society (ACS), 46
Anthony, Captain Aaron, 3, 4, 7–9, 10, 13, 15, 22. *See also* Wye House
Anti-Slavery Society, 47–52, 56, 68, 69, 70, 101
Apprentice, 33, 34, 63, 120
Auctions, slave, 5
Auld, Hugh, 15, 18, 19, 21, 32, 33, 34, 37, 58
Auld, Lucretia, 15, 22
Auld, Sophia, 15, 18–19, 21
Auld, Thomas, 15, 21–22, 37, 55, 58, 110
Auld, Tommy, 15, 18–19, 21
Aunt Katy, 10–12, 14
Autobiographies, 54–55, 57, 70, 112
Bailey, Betsey, 4, 6–7, 9
Bailey, Frederick Augustus Washington, 3, 55
Bailey, Harriet, 3–4, 10–12
Bailey, Henry, 30, 31
Bailey, Hester, 13
Bailey, Isaac, 4
Baltimore life, 16–22
  arriving in Baltimore, 16–18
  befriending white boys, 19
  duties, 18, 20, 33–34
  earning money, 20
  free blacks and, 35–37
  learning to read, 18–19, 20
  learning to write, 21

practicing speaking, 20
  reason for move to, 15
  return to, 32–33
  return to farm from, 22
Bankruptcy, 109, 120
Barbarians, 90, 120
Beatings, 1
  of Frederick, 24, 28, 34
  Frederick fighting back, 27–28
  of other slaves, 13, 24, 25
  slave breaker Covey and, 24–28
  telling world about, 53
Birth, of Frederick, 3
Black Code Laws, 100–101, 103
Black colony, 45–47
Black newspapers, 61
Black politicians, 105, 106
Brown, John, 68, 69, 77–78
Casualties, 94, 120
Cedar Hill, 111, 112, 116, 117
Children, of Frederick/Anna, 44, 56, 78, 113, 119
Civil rights, 103, 108, 114, 120
Civil War
  black soldiers in, 83, 88–91, 94, 95
  end of, 98–99
  Rebels and Yankees, 84
  rebuilding after, 96. *See also* Reconstruction
  start of, 81–82
Clothing allowance, of slaves, 11
Coffin, William C., 49–50
The Columbian Orator, 20
Commissions, 93, 120
Compromise, 72, 120
Compromise of 1850, 73
Confederacy, 80
Conspirators, 78, 120
Constitutional amendments, 93, 103–104, 114–115
Copybooks, 21, 120
Cornish, Samuel E., 61
Covey, Edward, 24–28
Cuffee, Paul, 46
Death, of Frederick, 117–119
Deep South, 24, 120
Diplomacy, 116, 120
Diplomat, in Haiti, 115–116

Douglass, Anna Murray
  death of, 113
  jobs, 47, 57
  Julia Griffiths scandal and, 67
  living abroad and, 58
  marriage to, 39–40
  meeting Frederick, 37
  raising family, 56–57, 63–64
  supporting Frederick, 64–65
Douglass, taking name of, 43
Dred Scott Decision, 73–75
Dresser, Amos, 49
Emancipation Proclamation, 85–87, 94
Fifth of July speech, 70–71
Fort Wagner, 94, 95
Freedmen's Bureau, 101–103
Freedom, 33–40
  autobiography threatening, 55
  blacks in Maryland, 35–37
  buying, 59
  fear of capture after, 38, 39, 40
  foiled escape and, 30–32
  Frederick wanting, 29–30, 34, 37–38
  manumission papers, 34, 59, 73, 120
  successful escape, 38–39
  Underground Railroad and, 75–76
Freedom's Journal, 61
Freeland farm experience, 28–32
Freeland, William, 28, 31
Fugitive Slave Act, 72–73, 75
Fugitive slave posters, 41
Garrison, William Lloyd, 50, 51, 86, 100–101, 111
  biographical sketch, 48
  concern about competing newspaper, 60
  differences with Frederick, 68–69
  Great Britain tour, 57
  inspiring Frederick, 45, 47
  introducing Frederick's first speech, 50
  The Liberator and, 45–47, 48, 51, 60

Garrison, William Lloyd (*cont*)
    touring with Frederick,
        53, 60
Grandmother. *See* Bailey,
    Betsey
Grant, Ulysses S., 98, 107–108
Great Britain
    buying freedom in, 59
    considering moving to,
        57–58
    return from, 60
    tour of, 56, 57–59
Griffiths, Julia, 59, 67
Harpers Ferry raid, 77–78
Harris, Henry and John, 28,
    30, 31
Hayes, Rutherford B., 114
Henny (cousin), 23, 24
Hodges, Willis, 61
Humiliating, 25, 120
Impeach, 107, 120
Investment, 70, 120
Investors, 62, 79, 109
James, Thomas, 45
Jenkins, Sandy, 28, 30, 31–32
Jim Crow laws, 115
Johnson, Andrew, 100,
    102–103, 107
Johnson, Frederick, 40
Johnson, Nathan and Mary,
    42–43
Ku Klux Klan, 106, 107
Lawson, Charles, 21
The Liberator, 45–47, 48, 51,
    60
*Life and Times of Frederick
    Douglass*, 112
Lincoln, Abraham. *See also*
    Civil War
        assassination of, 99
        Emancipation
            Proclamation and, 85–87,
            94
        Frederick meeting,
            92–93, 97–98
        inauguration reception,
            97–98
        presidential elections,
            78–80, 96
Lloyd, Colonel Edward, 7–9
Lloyd, Daniel, 14–15
Lobbying, 94, 120
Lynched/lynching, 107, 118,
    120
Manumission (papers), 34, 59,

73, 120
Marriages, of Frederick,
    39–40, 113–114
Massachusetts Anti-Slavery
    Society, 49–52
Misfortunes, series of,
    109–110
Mother. *See* Bailey, Harriet
Mott, Abigail and Lydia, 63–64
Mott, Lucretia Coffin, 64, 66
Murray, Anna. *See* Douglass,
    Anna Murray
My Bondage and My Freedom,
    70
Names, of Frederick, 3, 40, 43
*Narrative of the Life of Frederick
    Douglass*, 55, 57
New Bedford, 39, 42–45, 47,
    51, 64
Newspapers
    black, 61
    Frederick planning publica-
        tion, 59, 60
    The Liberator, 45–47, 48, 51,
        60
    North Star, 61, 62–63, 65,
        67, 69, 109
Orators, 20, 47, 53, 71, 120.
    See also Public speaking
Passes, for traveling slaves, 30,
    31
Pitts, Helen, 113–114, 116,
    119
Prejudice(d), 44, 52, 120
Progressive, 104, 120
Public speaking. *See also*
Orators
    angry mob incident, 52–53
    career beginning, 51
    demand for, 53
    Frederick beginning, 47–49
    at Massachusetts Anti-
        Slavery Society, 49–51
    people doubting truthful
        ness of, 54–55
    practicing as child, 20
    telling life story, 51, 53
Quakers, 46, 50, 120
The Ram's Horn, 61
Reading, learning and teaching,
    19, 20, 29
Reconstruction, 103–106,
    114–115, 120
Religion, 21, 45
Retaliation, 93, 120

Richardson family, 58–59
Roberts, Charles, 30, 31
Ruggles, David, 39, 40
Russwurm, John B., 61
Sabbath school, 28–29
Scandal, 67, 121
Scott, Dred, 73–75
Secession, 77, 80, 82, 121
Shipbuilding work, 33–34, 43
Slave auctions, 5
Slave breaker, 24–28
Slavery, of Frederick. *See also*
    Baltimore life; Beatings;
    Freedom
        birth, 3
        duties, 18, 20, 23, 33–34
        fear of being sold, 32, 37
        grandparent caretakers,
            3–6, 7, 9
        hired to Freeland farm,
            28–32
        hired to slave breaker,
            24–28
        Wye House and, 7–15
Slaves
    being sold, 5, 13–14, 23–24
    city vs. country, 17
    clothing allowance, 11
Slave trade, 2–3
Smith, Gerrit, 62, 79–80
Stanton, Edwin M., 92
Stanton, Elizabeth Cady, 66
Stowe, Harriet Beecher, 86, 87
Suffrage, 105, 121
Thirteenth Amendment, 94
Timeline, iv
Treason, 77, 121
Tubman, Harriet, 76
Turner, Nat, 25, 26
Uncle Tom's Cabin, 86, 87
Underground Railroad, 75–76
Veto(ed), 102, 103, 121
Violin, playing, 35
Voting rights, 104–106
Webster's spelling book, 20
Wells, Dr. Lewis G., 21
Wells, Ida B., 117, 118
Women's rights, 60, 65–66
World's Fair, 116, 121
Writing, learning, 21
Wye House, 7–15